NURTURING SPIRITUALITY IN CHILDREN

SIMPLE HANDS-ON ACTIVITIES

NURTURING SPIRITUALITY IN CHILDREN

PEGGY JOY JENKINS, Ph.D.

ATRIA BOOKS
New York London Toronto Sydney

BEYOND WORDS
PUBLISHING

ATRIA BOOKS

A Division of Simon & Schuster, Inc.
1230 Avenue of the Americas
New York, NY 10020

BEYOND WORDS
PUBLISHING

20827 N.W. Cornell Road, Suite 500
Hillsboro, Oregon 97124-9808
503-531-8700 / 503-531-8773 fax
www.beyondword.com

Managing editor: Lindsay S. Brown
Copyeditor: Gretchen Stelter
Proofreader: Robert Vaughn
Design: Sara E. Blum
Composition: William H. Brunson Typography Services

First Atria Books/Beyond Words trade paper edition July 2008

ATRIA BOOKS and colophon are trademarks of Simon & Schuster, Inc. Beyond Words Publishing is a division of Simon & Schuster, Inc.

For more information about special discounts for bulk purchases, please contact Simon & Schuster Special Sales at 1-800-456-6798 or business@simonandschuster.com.

Manufactured in the United States of America

10 9 8 7 6 5 4 3 2

Library of Congress Cataloging-in-Publication Data:

Jenkins, Peggy Davison.
    Nurturing spirituality in children : simple hands-on activities / Peggy Joy Jenkins. — 1st Atria Books/Beyond Words trade paper ed.
        p. cm.
Includes indexes.
    1. Religious education of young people. 2. Youth—Religious life. I. Title.

BL42.J46   2008
204'.41—dc22

2007050937

ISBN-13: 978-1-58270-211-7
ISBN-10:   1-58270-211-X

The corporate mission of Beyond Words Publishing, Inc.: *Inspire to Integrity*

CONTENTS

SEEDLINGS

FOR THE BEGINNING LEARNER

SPROUTS

FOR THE MORE ADVANCED LEARNER

FULL BLOOM

FOR THE EXPERIENCED LEARNER

ACKNOWLEDGMENTS

First, I must acknowledge the powerful guidance of the set of books called A *Course in Miracles*. Next, I owe a debt of gratitude to the many ministers, teachers, and authors who have provided the inspiration for many of the lessons in this book. Over my years of study, the ideas and sources have blended into a whole, making it difficult for me to give isolated credit. Nevertheless, my gratitude goes to everyone who contributed to this work.

I am deeply grateful to both Prentice-Hall and Coleman Publishing for their vision in printing earlier editions of this book and to Beyond Words for their awareness that it was time to reintroduce the book to the world.

Nothing of this nature is ever achieved alone, so I acknowledge with great appreciation all the invisible help I received, by whatever name one chooses to call it.

PREFACE

This book is a revision of my earlier work, *A Child of God*. I have found that many people who believe in a Prime Creator, Great Spirit, etc., are not comfortable with the word God. Therefore, I have de-emphasized that word, and I invite people to substitute their favorite terminology. These lessons are based on universal principles—principles that hold true no matter what the country, culture, or religion.

With my background as a mother, parent/teacher educator, and student of spiritual and universal principles, I felt it was only logical to bring these fields together in the hope of accelerating the consciousness growth our world needs. As a parent, I felt a great need for more information on mental and spiritual principles in a form easy to share with children. The result was the combination of two favorite teaching tools—visual aids and analogies—to teach children the principles of truth.

The saying *we teach what we need to learn* never felt truer to me than when I was writing this book. I am joyous about sharing it with you, and I hope that it may help you as it has helped me. It is certainly not a book just for teaching children, but for teaching the child in each of us.

It is my loving hope that you and the children on your path have a joyful time as you journey through these lessons.

Great truths are dearly bought.
The common truth,
Such as men give and take from day to day,
Comes in the common walk of easy life,
Blown by the careless wind across our way.
Great truths are greatly won, not found by chance,
Nor wafted on the breath of summer's dream,
But grasped in the great struggle of the soul,
By hard buffeting with adverse wind and stream.

Unknown

LAYING THE FOUNDATION

*"The child must rise to the higher order of
the spirit through concrete things."*
—Dr. Maria Montessori

A goal of this book is to help young people start believing
the things that are true about themselves as children of the
Creator. When they know these truths, fantastic things begin
to happen to them and to their world.

Someone once said, "Woe to the man who has to learn principles in the time of crisis." The principles children learn from
this book will help prepare them for whatever they may
encounter, because they will understand that theirs is a mental
and spiritual world and that whatever is in their lives is the
material expression of their beliefs. Many people see the outside world as cause and themselves as effect. I hope children
will come to see themselves as cause and the world as effect.
Then they will provide the leadership needed to usher in a
new era.

For every physical law, there is a parallel law in mind and
spirit. Teaching children to work with the spiritual laws, as
well as the physical ones, will bring them the gifts of peace,
confidence, and joy, which will enable them to weather the
storms of life.

The lessons that follow are simply to start the process. They are intended as aids for busy parents who are willing to take ten minutes a day to teach higher principles to their children. Many teachers, spiritual leaders, and counselors will find them useful too. The lessons do not represent all the principles that need to be taught. They are simply those that meet the criteria of being quick to teach with common objects at the level of understanding of most school-age children.

The highest kinds of learning happen via symbols, not words, and easy-to-understand objects can symbolize many hard-to-understand truths. Common objects have long been used to make the unfamiliar clear. These lessons, therefore, use the concrete to support the abstract.

You do not need to know all the answers to use these lessons. Just set the stage and tickle the children with these concepts, which their Inner Teachers can mold into perfect understanding.

Throughout the book, I have tried to be as nondenominational as possible. Although I use words such as God, Spirit, Source, the Creator, and Inner Teacher, please realize that these words are only labels. Language attempts to define what is indefinable. These words are attempts to describe what each of us knows in our hearts, our souls. Let these words mean whatever your beliefs are. Feel free to change them to suit your beliefs.

You needn't be in full agreement with this book, but if the ideas trigger your thinking and give you other ideas for teaching truths that are meaningful to you, the book will have served its purpose.

HOW TO USE THIS BOOK

"Brain research shows that 83 percent of what we learn
is through seeing and doing."
—Dr. Edward de Bono

The best formula for using these lessons is KISS (Keep It Short and Simple). Short and simple makes for a more lasting impression. Children's minds really don't need a lot of words and explanations. Adults' minds do!

There is no sequence to the lessons. Treat the book as a smorgasbord or buffet and pick and choose lessons depending on your child's needs and your interests. Watch for "teachable" moments.

These lessons are adaptable to any age group from elementary through high school. Even if young people of diverse age groups are hearing a lesson together, they will "get it" at their levels of understanding. That is why I have not included scripts or explanations for specific age levels.

Offer explanations that correspond to your child's age and level of understanding. Since these lessons pertain to different levels of awareness, it is OK to alter or eliminate any that are not entirely accurate according to your philosophy. It is much better to teach the lessons you are excited about. This kind of enthusiasm is contagious. With children, much more is "caught than taught."

The dialogue in the lessons is not intended to be read directly to your child. Use it as a starting point for your own thinking, and augment it with examples familiar to your child.

Studies show that children have greater retention when tasks are left incomplete. So it's better to cut the lessons short, letting them want a little more, than to exhaust the subject and bore them. Just plan to revisit the idea occasionally.

Most lessons can be accomplished in five minutes or so. I suggest adding the lessons to your morning schedule because the mind, as well as the body, needs to be nourished. Otherwise, use the lessons at afterschool snack-time, dinnertime, or bedtime. Try to have a regular schedule and to be consistent.

Read each lesson at least three days before you present it; this is for a couple of reasons. One, by reading ahead of time, you will be sure you have whatever objects you need. Most items are common to every household, but now and then there are a few exceptions. Two, by reading the lessons ahead of time, you will give your creative subconscious valuable time with the principle behind the lesson, which may provide you with examples your child will relate to. You'll also have a deeper understanding of the principle by the time you give the lesson and, perhaps, a more meaningful way to present it. Please keep in mind that this material is intended to be open-ended, so you can present it in a way that is most in keeping with your belief system while best meeting the needs of your child.

Before a lesson begins, make sure you have all the objects you'll need on a table. Covering them with a cloth may provide a bit of mystery, maybe even suspense. You may designate a special tray or mat for the lessons. Using a puppet or two to help teach the lessons is a most effective way to enhance the drama.

Be sure to allow time for the children's discussion and questions. Try not to make lessons into monologues. Often children are closer to the truth than we are and can teach us with their keen insights. Be willing to reverse roles and be the learner.

Sometimes it may be impossible or inappropriate to use the objects suggested for a lesson, but it's still best to use props to help you get the message across. Instead of objects, you may use pictures or "paint" word pictures. When children use their imaginations, they create much more lasting impressions than if they use words without visual images. A hands-on experience with objects will always make the strongest impression, however, so use props whenever possible. It is reported that we remember 10 percent of what we hear, 25 percent of what we see, and 90 percent of what we do.

Another way of retaining information is through spaced repetition. A principle may need to be repeated many times before it is retained, so repeat some of the lessons every so often. Many of the lessons are simply different ways of saying the same thing, and that is also effective teaching.

Throughout each lesson, it is of utmost importance to build the children's self-esteem. The goal of the lesson is never more important than the feelings of the children. Always help the children to feel good about themselves. This is best encompassed succinctly by the phrase, "We teach what we are and what others are to us."

After each lesson you will see an affirmation, which you can use to end the session. Affirmations are positive declarations of truth and, as such, are powerful tools for changing one's thinking and attitudes, and hence, for changing one's experiences. They are more fully explained in the section "Guidelines for Affirmations." The affirmations are usually an outgrowth of each lesson. They can directly reinforce the lesson or relate to concerns that were revealed when the children discussed the lesson. Repeating affirmations throughout the day can help children become closer to truths about themselves.

To make this book a more effective teaching tool: Keep a separate notebook to record ideas before, during, and after each lesson; Include your plans for augmenting the lesson (for example, with role-playing, meditations, and art and science projects); Record how the children received the lesson, and make suggestions for using it next time. Your categories could include the following:

1. Lesson title
2. Date used
3. Additions to the lesson
4. Alterations to the lesson
5. Examples to offer
6. Other affirmation ideas
7. Children's responses and questions
8. Activities to augment the lesson
9. Suggestions for using the lesson again

Perhaps the greatest contribution these lessons can make will be to trigger similar ideas you can use to better portray your philosophy. I hope these activities will be a jumping-off point and that you'll start seeing many ways to expand children's understanding of their mental and spiritual universe in everyday objects.

I hear-I forget
I see-I remember
I do-I understand

Chinese proverb

GUIDELINES FOR AFFIRMATIONS

An affirmation concludes each lesson, so I suggest you read this section before you begin the lessons.

Affirmations, as used in this book, are positive statements about who we are and what we can become or experience. They are useful as agents of change—as tools for bringing about the change we want in our thinking and experience. This change is in our beliefs about ourselves. We need to bring our self-awareness into harmony with the divine perfection that already exists within us.

Our beliefs are stored in the subconscious areas of our minds. They are made up of emotions, fears, doubts, actual happenings, and the accepted opinions of others. They accept negative thoughts just as easily as they accept positive thoughts, and they create what we feel is true for us. Here is where the tool of using affirmations comes in. Affirmations can help us counteract some of the negatives we've told ourselves or accepted from others. Because we are spirit, we are, in essence, perfect. We have a right to call forth that perfection.

Affirmations work very rapidly with young children because children are close to the truth about themselves. They have not had as many years of "brainwashing" as most adults have. We adults have unconsciously used negative affirmations most of our lives, bringing about many unwanted conditions. We affirm negatively when we say, "I can't do this;" "I'm so tired;" "I think I'm getting sick;" "I'm such a slow reader;" "I'm lousy at spelling;" or "My memory is poor." Usually this kind of affirming, or self-negation, is carried on silently in our "self-talk" (that steady stream of internal verbalization).

Almost anything we really want to change about ourselves can be changed by using positive declarations or affirmations. They help counteract the bombardment of self-inflicted put-downs we experience throughout the day. Affirmations clothed with feeling have the power to impregnate our subconscious minds through the process of osmosis, just like a stalk of celery that turns red when it sits in red-colored water and absorbs it. Other useful analogies are in the lesson "The Power of Affirmations."

Affirmations must be believable to our conscious minds before they will be fully accepted by our subconscious minds. The subconscious parts of our minds have formative power. That is, they will give form to what we feel is true for us now. It is the feelings, not the words, that give rise to the form.

Suggestions for Forming Affirmations

Make the affirmation personal by using "I," "My," or your name. Powerful affirmations begin with "I am." "I can" affirmations are also very effective.

Word your affirmation as if you have already made the change you want to make, as if you are already the kind of person you want to be.

Use present tense, because future tense can destroy the value of an affirmation. The subconscious mind is very literal, and if your affirmation is worded to take place in the future, it will always be in the future. Avoid "I will...," "I am getting...," and similar statements.

Your affirmation should indicate that you have achieved the result, not that you are "growing into it."

Affirmations work best if accompanied by mental pictures. It is easier to picture an accomplished fact than a vague process of growth.

Your affirmation should describe the attitudes you wish to cultivate not what you want to move away from. Use positives, not negatives. Instead of "I don't lose my temper," say, "I am even-tempered."

Do not compare yourself with others in your affirmation, such as "I can write as well as Susan." Focus on yourself: "I express myself clearly."

Be specific as to the exact level you want to achieve: "I can swim three laps of the pool" or "I can play this week's piano lesson perfectly."

Inject feeling words into your affirmations to give them an emotional charge: "I enjoy doing math" or "I am proud of my computer skills."

Suggestions for Using Affirmations

The most important affirmations for children are those that build their self-esteem. Self-esteem is the foundation of joyful, successful lives. Many parents and teachers teach their small children to use the magic words "I like myself." Such words foster friendliness and cooperation because we must first like ourselves in order to like others. Encourage the children to use these magic words three times when they wake up and when they're about to go to sleep in order to counteract the bombardment of put-downs from self and others that they may experience throughout the day.

Older children can use "I feel warm and loving toward myself" or "I love myself totally and completely." The "self" referred to is the Higher Self, and these words mean that the children are affirming the Spirit within them.

I urge you to use affirmative prayer before you begin the day's object lesson. Before coming together with the children, write or say something like, "The minds and hearts of these children are open to receive the lesson at their levels of understanding."

Affirmations impress our subconscious mind most powerfully if they are used when we are in a very relaxed state, such as when falling asleep, waking up, or meditating. That is why many parents speak affirmations softly to their children while they are falling asleep. That is also why negative thoughts held at such times can do so much damage. For this reason, you may wish to make sure that your children don't fall asleep while listening to the radio or television.

The formative subconscious mind is very receptive to detailed visualization, so a mental picture accompanying the affirmation is extremely effective. A strong picture can be worth a thousand words.

The more joyous the emotion you attach to the affirmation, the more effective the affirmation will be. Feelings, both negative and positive, have formative power.

Repetition is another key to successful affirming. Use it many times each day. Display the affirmation in several places as a helpful reminder, and change the places frequently.

The more senses you involve, the more power you will add to your affirmation. For rapid results, I recommend writing it, speaking it, chanting it, singing it, and dancing it.

SEEDLINGS

FOR THE BEGINNING LEARNER

1
THE STRAW SMILE

This lesson is a good exercise to do before each of the other lessons.

Materials
Any kind of drinking straw.

Lesson
"Breathe in. Now put your straw in your mouth, between your teeth; don't let it touch the lips. Now leave it just like that while I explain what we're doing. This is called the 'Straw Smile.' Stress reduction research shows that if you do this for a full three minutes, you release endorphins (the feel-good hormones) from the brain cells.

"I will talk to you for the three minutes, and you keep the straw between your teeth. These endorphins are also released when you laugh. Laughter does so many good things for our bodies. Here's a few: it increases oxygen levels in the cells, which gives you energy; it stimulates the immune system of the body; and it's beneficial for anxiety, insomnia, irritability, depression, asthma, tension, migraine headaches, and many other aches and pains.

"Laughter is called internal jogging because it provides a good massage to all internal organs. It might seem silly to hold these straws like this, but notice that it is making your face smile; science has shown that even if you don't feel happy, if you hold a smile on your face for a while and act happy, you actually do become more happy."

You might want to think about having straws in clean places all over your house and in your car.

End this lesson with a long and hearty laugh.

Suggested Affirmation
I am a joyful person and laugh often.

2
THE MAGNETISM
OF PRAISE

Materials

A saucer of sand and a magnet or two. (Salt with some iron filings added may be substituted. Test with the magnet to make sure you have enough iron. If necessary you can add iron to the sand by filing slivers off an iron nail.) Optional: a magnifying glass.

Lesson

Ask the children if they can pick out the tiny particles of iron that are in the sand with their eyes or fingers. Ask what tool could help them do that. Bring out a magnet and watch the specks of iron stick to it.

"The saucer of sand [or salt] represents your day, and the magnet represents a thankful heart. A thankful heart can scan your day and pick out many blessings, just as the magnet can pick out the iron. But an ungrateful heart is like your fingers. It can search and search through the sand—your day—and not find any iron particles or anything to praise. A heart that is full of thankfulness and praise will find something to be grateful for in every hour of the day."

Suggest taking turns picking up particles of iron with the magnet. Pretend that they are the blessings each child has had during the hour. Friends, eyesight, hearing, a good breakfast, and nice clothing may be examples of blessings they think of.

Another sweep with the magnet can pick up blessings they received during the previous hour, such as compliments, family members, playthings, and pets. Continue sweeping with the magnet through previous hours, even through the previous day.

Explain that whenever we show gratitude for what is in our lives, the gratitude works like a magnet and draws more good things to us. This appreciation may be silent and may take the form of silently praising the fine qualities we see in others. Such praise will magnetize those qualities to us, and we'll have even more to be thankful for.

This analogy could be applied to a current challenge in a child's life, such as a move to a new state or a broken leg. The saucer of sand represents the situation, the magnet the mind that searches for the good in it, and the iron particles the blessings the child can discover.

For an additional analogy, bring out a magnifying glass and explain that Spirit magnifies what we praise and bless. Those blessings represented by the particles of iron will increase when we have a truly thankful heart. What we think about expands.

Suggested Affirmation
I am a grateful person, and I enjoy praising the good in my life.

3
FINDING OUR WAY

Materials
Rocks from hiking trail.

Lesson
There are many things that help keep us on the right path when we are hiking through the woods, desert, or anywhere out in nature. Where I live, hikers and forest rangers make piles of, usually, flat rocks to mark the route of a trail. In the high desert you could easily get lost without these "sign posts" along the trail. Another way to keep on the right trail is to watch for the rock formations (such as arrow shapes) left behind by friends who proceeded you.

"We are on a trail called Life, and we can get off the path easily without guidance. What kind of guidance, prayers, or listening within do you use?" Discuss when you might need help to get back on the path. What can you do if you feel lost? (Here is a good place for the adults to share their methods of getting guidance.)

Suggested Affirmation
I can connect with the Spirit within and always know what I am to do.

4

THE INSIDE GIVES FORM
TO THE OUTSIDE

Materials

One or two inflated balloons and three or four balloons that haven't been blown up. Optional: a balloon for each child.

Lesson

"The Invisible Shapes the Visible" is another name for this lesson. Begin by explaining that each balloon represents a person, and that each person is filled with the breath of life, just like the balloons are when they are blown up. Suggest that the children blow up the balloons by filling them with their breaths of life. Help them to see that the air, or life, is in all balloons and all people.

"People see only the outside of the balloon or the outside of people, and they tend to think that's the important part. What's really important, however, is what is on the inside, because what's on the inside creates the outside. It's the inside that gives form to the balloon. Otherwise, it would be limp and useless, like one of the balloons that is still empty." Show the children the balloons you haven't blown up.

"We need to know that the insides of others are more important than their outside forms. The air inside us is important because it is what gives us life. Our thoughts and feelings are also important things that are inside of us. In many ways, these things help shape us and our experiences. What is most important is the Spirit within." (You may prefer to substitute other terminology for this point of perfection that all people share despite their outward appearances.)

Continue with the balloon analogy: "Can you see that the life, or air, on the inside of the balloon is the important part? What happens to the air when you release it from the balloon?" The children will see that the air rejoins the air outside the balloon.

You may want to compare the release of air, or life, to the death of the body. Help the children see that there is no real death because the life force rejoins its source, just like the air does, and continues on in a different form. If there has been a recent death in the family, this could be a most helpful lesson.

Suggested Affirmation

I remember that what's inside people is more important than what's outside.

5
WE ARE A VISIBLE FORM OF SPIRIT

Materials
A bowl of cold water with ice cubes in it.

Lesson
Explain that the ice cubes represent all people, and the water represents Spirit, the invisible power of the universe. Water can take solid form, which is, of course, how we get ice. Spirit, which is invisible, can also take form and become visible. We are visible forms of Spirit, just as the ice cubes are another form of water.

Explain that the ice cubes originally came from water rather than the water from the ice cubes. We came forth from the invisible to the visible, and like the ice when it melts and becomes water once again, at the time of so-called death, we simply lay aside our bodies, and our spirits return to Spirit, or the so-called invisible.

To allay fears about being invisible, or "nothing," explain that when our spirits return to Spirit, we'll be in a world that will be very happy, comfortable, and visible. We'll simply be in spiritual bodies instead of physical bodies. Explain that some people aren't immediately aware that they have left their physical bodies when they have made the transition called death. Consider looking into some of the current books on life after death. Your librarian can help you.

End the lesson by explaining that everything is energy, but it changes form, just as water can change from liquid to ice or steam. A steaming teakettle on the stove can emphasize this change of form.

Suggested Affirmation
I am a spiritual being in physical form.

6
JOY LIGHTS

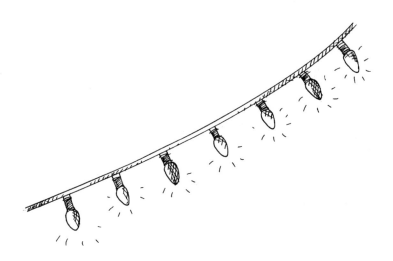

Materials

A pretty string of Christmas or holiday lights.

Lesson

The spirit within is like sparkling holiday tree lights. The child in each of us enjoys the beauty of strings of colored lights, whether over the fireplace, around a doorway, or on a patio. Don't wait for the holiday. When you turn on the switch, the festive light ignites the spirit of joy within.

Consider having a short string of lights on a wall where your child can plug it in to remember a connection to joy and light. Or you can turn it on frequently as an example of how can let God into our lives. It can be a symbol for the peace, ve, and joy in our hearts.

Life can be heavy, but all we need to do is turn a switch in our heart, and only a few minutes later, Life sparkles. Let the sparkling lights remind you of your inner Light.

This lesson can be extended for days by using the colorful bulbs as symbols of new ideas.

Suggested Affirmation

My spirit within is sparkling like holiday lights.

7
PRAYER MAKES THE DAY

Materials

A loosely woven piece of fabric about six inches square or larger. One edge should be hemmed and the opposite edge frayed a bit. Optional: a piece of cloth that is not hemmed and a needle and thread for each child.

Lesson

This lesson is based on a quote from an unknown author:

"A day hemmed with prayer is less likely to unravel."

Point out how the hem is preventing the edge of the cloth from unraveling. Pull a loose thread from the opposite end to show what can happen to a cloth without a hem. You might even compare a fully hemmed piece of fabric with a piece that is not hemmed at all, after each has gone through the washing machine.

The hem represents prayer, especially early-morning prayer. The fabric is our day, and the unraveled edge of the fabric represents the troubles, irritants, and mistakes that can occur in our day. The children can offer examples of a day that is full of "goofs."

Offer examples of prayer that can be used to start a day on the right foot, including asking for guidance through the day, affirming divine order for the day, affirming to be helpful to others, and affirming a state of peace and love no matter what occurs. With needle and thread, the children can hem their pieces of cloth while they contribute affirmative prayer thoughts. Or the children could memorize a short prayer that is appropriate for their ages, such as "I am a Spirit in action in all I think, say, and do today," or "Spirit in me thinks through me, feels through me, and acts through me today."

Here you could discuss the powerful technique of visualizing a happy day. Practice it together on a simple and specific thought.

Here are some other ideas you could use with older children:

Because a thought joined with a feeling has creative power, maybe we're praying all day long.

This is a free-will planet, so we have to ask for what we want. The spiritual realm can't interfere with our free will.

Prayer is often thought of as talking to Spirit, meditation as listening to Spirit.

If we are asking for spiritual guidance, how foolish it would be not to take time to quiet our minds and listen for an answer.

Suggested Affirmation
Prayer starts my day, and I let Spirit lead the way.

8
OUR RELATIONSHIP
TO SPIRIT

Materials

A loaf of bread without slices cut but with pieces of various sizes and shapes torn from it. An unfrosted angel food cake also works. If you are working with one or two children, use a roll.

Lesson

Give each child a piece of bread. "Do your pieces look the same? Even though they are different sizes and shapes, what is the same about them?" Help them to see that each piece of bread contains identical ingredients. One piece doesn't have more salt, another more flour.

Explain that the pieces of bread are just like us. We are made up of the same basic stuff even though our shapes and sizes are different. The loaf of bread represents Spirit, or God, and because Spirit is everywhere present, it is in each of us. We all are a small part of Spirit, and so have within us the divine qualities of peace, joy, clarity, love, health, order, wisdom, power, and so forth.

Discuss how this is true of everybody in the world. No matter what people look like or act like, we all have the qualities of Spirit inside us. But these qualities are well hidden in some people, because they don't know about them. We can help those people by looking for the love, peace, order, health, and goodness we know is in them. We are all part of Spirit; there is no separation.

You could expand this idea to include animals and plants.

Suggested Affirmation
As a child of Spirit, I have the qualities of Spirit.

9
THE BOOMERANG LAW

Materials
A rubber band. Optional: a boomerang, a yo-yo, or a party horn that unrolls when it's blown and then rolls back.

Lesson
The boomerang law is another name for the law of cause and effect, a basic law that is known by many different labels. The aim of this lesson is to remind us that we will reap what we sow—that what goes around comes around.

Have the children observe while you put a rubber band around your finger, stretch it, and let it lightly snap back. Do this a few times. "The law of cause and effect says that what goes out comes back—just like the rubber band did. Whatever is put into the universe, by thought, word, or action, travels back to the central point that sent it out. So, if we send friendly thoughts and actions out, we will attract friendliness from others." Pull the rubber band to represent a friendly thought about someone. Now let it lightly snap back to represent a good thought returning as a result of the friendly thought. Next have the children choose a critical thought about someone. Pull the rubber band out and let it snap back to indicate that criticism will also return to them.

If you are using a yo-yo, toss it out and name a positive thought like love. As the yo-yo returns, say "love" again to represent love coming back. Repeat this with a negative example as well.

"As ye sow, so shall ye reap" is another way of stating the boomerang law. If we are sharing and helpful, we'll find people eager to share with us and give us a hand. If we hold fearful thoughts or act as if we are afraid of getting hurt or losing something, sure enough, those kinds of experiences will come into our world.

End on a positive note by emphasizing the children's fantastic, creative natures and their ability to choose what comes into their lives through their thoughts and feelings. An action is always preceded by a thought and a feeling.

Suggested Affirmation
Only good goes from me, and only good comes to me.

10
WE ARE ALL CONNECTED

Materials

A variety of beads or buttons with two or four holes (not shanks) and a long piece of cord or string. With a group of children, use individual strings; alternatively, for a very large group of children, each child in the group could add beads to one very long string.

Lesson

In this lesson, the cord represents Spirit, or God; the beads are our individuality, or our individualization of Spirit; and the colors, shapes, and textures represent our different personalities and appearances.

Have the children choose beads or buttons to place on the string and name a person that each bead represents, such as Dad, Uncle Charlie, Nana, baby sister, teacher, mail carrier, and themselves. Each bead or button should have a different feel and look, just as each person does.

Lead the children to see that all these people have something in common—a common thread at the center of their beings. This cord, which connects us like the string connects all the buttons or beads, could be called Spirit. People have many names for it, and it is at the center of everyone. Make sure they know you are not talking about the center of the physical body.

"It is good to look beyond the beads' colors and shapes or beyond people's different appearances and personalities, and to know that way inside, at the center or core of us, we are all the same. This core is perfect and is the most important part of us. If we look at people as if they are like the beads with different colors and shapes, we can feel very separate and different from others. But if we remember that we are all connected by the cord of Spirit, we can feel close to others. We can choose to look for this center of perfection within people, rather than looking at just the outer person."

If appropriate, take a few minutes for the children to still their minds, go within, and feel that cord of love, peace, and perfection.

Suggested Affirmation
I look for the perfection in others.

11
JUDGE NOT

This lesson may be divided into two parts.

Materials

Part 1: A small portion of a picture from a magazine, calendar, or advertisement flyer for each child. For instance, if the picture is of a face, cut out the mouth for one child, an eye for another child, a piece of cheek, chin, or ear for another child, and so on. If the picture is of nature, just cut out a tree or a bit of a lake.

Part 2: A sheet of white paper with a small hole punched in the middle for each child. The children may punch it themselves with a pencil or it may be pre-punched.

Lesson

Part 1: Hand each child a piece of the picture and ask them all to give opinions about what the whole picture is. They'll find this task to be just a guessing game. They will see that they don't have enough facts to make an accurate judgment. Explain that this is true about most judgments we make in this world, especially those regarding people.

Hold up a picture of an ear or a nose. "Just as we can't tell much about this face from this small bit of information, we really can't tell much about people from their appearances or actions. To judge people rightly, we would have to know so much about their past and their present that a fair judgment would be impossible. All we see are bits of anything, never the whole picture, so we need to give up thinking that we under-stand the whole thing from these bits. Understanding this concept is wisdom, and wisdom is not judgment."

Part 2: Hand the children sheets of paper and ask them to punch small holes in the center to peek through. "Look through the hole at me and tell me how much you can see. Look around the room; see how your vision is limited by the size of the hole?

"Most of us are looking at the world only through peepholes. Our vision of other people is peephole vision. Get close to one another and look at each other through your peepholes. Just as you are able to see only a fragment of one another through the hole, this is also all you're really seeing or understanding of any other person or of any situation. All of humanity's awareness at the level of development we are at here on earth is very limited. Therefore, we need to be very careful that we're not judging people or situations. We just don't see the whole pic-ture. We don't have sufficient awareness.

"Only the Creator's judgment is perfect. Only by staying open-minded will we be able to tune in to that level of awareness. When our minds are made up, it is impossible to hear Spirit within us. We can ask for wisdom in any situation, and then we can go into the silence and listen for guidance." The lesson might close with a guided listening meditation preceded by some deep breathing for relaxation.

Suggested Affirmation

I let go of judgment and rely on the wisdom of the Spirit within.

12
THE HARD WAY VERSUS THE EASY WAY

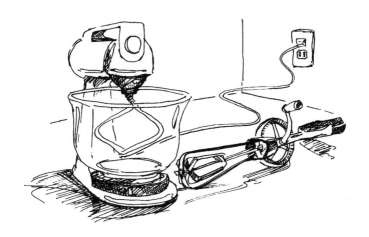

Materials
A whisk and an electric beater.

Lesson
Demonstrate how both the whisk and electric beater do much the same thing, but with one it's much harder work. Allow the children to try both by helping you whip some soap flakes in water, egg whites, or whipping cream. Lead them to see how much easier the electric beater is for whipping.

"Using the whisk for a long time can be exhausting. It is harder to use because it is detached from power. The electric beater is easy because it is attached to power. The cord and the electrical outlet are channels for the electrical power.

"The same is true with people. We have a choice of using the higher power, Spirit power, or of not using it and going it alone. If we go it alone, we become exhausted and have unsatisfactory results. But when we ask for the help of Spirit, we tap into the source of all love, wisdom, and knowledge. We can receive guidance that is just right for our particular project and we can receive the energy to see it through.

"If we know there is a higher power, a spiritual power, that we can use but choose not to, it's like knowing how to read but not reading. It's like having the instruction manual for a piece of equipment but trying to figure out how to use it without reading the instructions. So, would you rather make toast with a toaster or a candle?

"Through prayer, or silent sitting, we can tune in to the higher power. Simply ask for help or guidance and then quiet your mind and listen for what you are to do next."

End the lesson with a short listening meditation.

Suggested Affirmation
I turn to a higher power for guidance.

13
CUT YOUR PROBLEM
IN HALF

This lesson (and many others) can be effectively offered using puppets. If one puppet is used, the dialogue is carried on between you and the puppet.

Materials
A potato or a lump of clay, a small cutting board, and a knife.

Lesson
Welcoming problems without resentment cuts the problems in half.

"Life is a schoolhouse, full of wonderful lessons to be learned from the problems we encounter. Our attitudes toward these problems are part of our lesson. Our attitudes can make learning fun or not fun.

"The potato [or lump of clay] represents a problem, any kind of problem you may have. I know a way to make that problem smaller, a way to cut it down to half its size." First, ask for ideas from the children. They may have great thoughts for making problems or challenges seem smaller. Then share that one way to cut a problem in half is to cut out or remove the resentment from it.

Demonstrate by cutting the potato in half. Label the removed part *Resentment*, and show that this resentment is what made the problem seem twice its size. "When we let go of those feelings of annoyance and bless the problem, not only will it seem smaller, but we will have freed our energy so we can look for solutions. Resentment, like all negative emotions, is a form of fear, and it blocks our energy.

"When you learn to welcome your problems as interesting challenges, as opportunities for learning, as simply the lessons that life is giving you, all your problems will seem half the size. And you never need to be alone in dealing with a problem or with resentment. The Creator is always available and can be asked for help. Spirit can turn resentment into love."

Suggested Affirmation
I accept my problems as exciting challenges and release resentful feelings.

14
WATCH YOUR WORDS

Materials

A bowl of water, a salt shaker or a small dish of salt, and a teaspoon.

Lesson

This lesson shows that words, once spoken, cannot be taken back, at least not on the physical plane. We can reverse their effects, however, through prayer and positive action.

"The small dish [or salt shaker] represents us, the salt is our words, and the bowl of water is another person." Shake the salt into the water. "See how the words have dissolved in the other person if the other person accepts them?" Personalize the demonstration by telling how you had an argument with someone and used names you were sorry about afterward. As you sprinkle salt over the water, explain, "These are the words I used: stupid, lazy, liar, crazy, loser. Afterward, I wanted to take them back because I didn't really mean them. But do you think I could? Could you get some of those words or salt grains out of the water for me?

"Our words and thoughts go out into the ocean of thought around us, and just like the salt, they can never be retrieved. Therefore, it is very important to think carefully about what we say. Before speaking, we can ask ourselves if what we are about to say would help the thought atmosphere or pollute it, if it would create joy or pain for the other person.

"The same is true of thoughts as well as words. We can help neutralize negative thoughts by substituting positive, constructive affirmations. For example, we can withdraw a thought of someone as a loser by thinking of that person as a winner. How might we lessen the saltiness, the negativity, in our bowl of water? Will this work with the thought atmosphere?"

Positive declarations can dilute a lot of negativity. Explain that all our mistakes can be corrected on the spiritual level by Spirit. Remember that children must not be left with a sense of guilt. Teach that through affirmations and prayer we can heal past errors and feel forgiven.

Suggested Affirmation
I carefully monitor my words and thoughts.

15
OUR HIDDEN
POTENTIAL

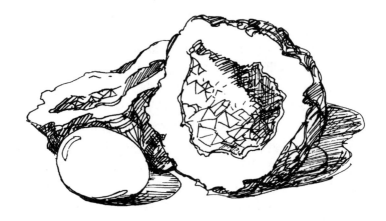

**This lesson includes two separate analogies,
so you may want to do them at different times.**

Materials

A raw egg, a small glass dish, and a geode (a half will do, but
two halves taped together is more fun).

Lesson

Part 1: Hold up the egg and talk about what a miracle it is.
Say that we are just as much of a miracle. "If some people
came from a country that had no eggs, do you think they
would believe that a chicken could come out of this shell?"

Break the egg into the dish. "Those people would examine the contents for traces of feathers, eyes, or legs, and then they would surely decide there was no potential life in such a gooey mess. Yet, if a fertile egg is kept warm for an appropriate amount of time, the contents within the shell will turn themselves into a perfect chick.

"It is the same with us. Our potential, our hidden splendor, doesn't show up unless it is acknowledged and nurtured. Parents can help, but we must learn to do this for ourselves. We, too, already contain everything necessary to be all that Spirit designed us to be. We are complete and perfect, but like the baby chick, we must be willing to break out of our shells. It's a solo act. Nobody can do it for us."

Part 2: The second analogy is portrayed by a geode, those unattractive grayish rocks that, when cut open, reveal gorgeous crystals of different colors. Show the taped geode. "This is symbolic of us. The rough edges and blotches represent the shortcomings we see—our mistakes, our bad habits."

Then separate the rock halves or turn over the one half to expose the inside. "Just as there is unexpected light and beauty within the dull rock, so there is unexpected light, love, and genius within each of us. This is our true nature, our real self, and it is what we want to identify with, not our outer self."

The metamorphosis of caterpillar to chrysalis to butterfly would also make an appropriate analogy for this lesson.

Suggested Affirmation

I accept the magnificence within me and let my words and actions reflect my true identity.

16
SPIRIT IS PRESENT EVERYWHERE

Materials
A clear glass or plastic bowl filled with water and a tiny clear glass bottle without a lid.

Lesson
The illustration above represents the body totally immersed in Spirit. But who or what Spirit is can be confusing for young children. One day they hear that Spirit is within: "Go within and listen to Spirit in your heart." The next day they hear that Spirit is everywhere and in everything, even the cockroach.

This simple visual analogy can make a complex subject very clear. The water represents pure Spirit, and it is both inside and outside the body, which is represented by the little glass bottle. If the children have seen the ocean, compare the bowl of water to the ocean and the little bottle to their bodies, or tell them that we are all like drops of water in the huge ocean of Spirit. When we recognize this, we can accept that divine love and wisdom is always available to us. We are never alone.

You may wish to refer back to the analogy of the loaf of bread, which showed how we are all fragments of the whole, with the same divine qualities.

Suggested Affirmation

There is not a spot where God is not.

17
I'LL SEE IT WHEN
I BELIEVE IT

Materials

A catalog or two.

Lesson

"The law of deliberate creation says there must be a balance between wanting and expecting in order for us to create something new in our lives. For instance, if we want to go to camp, we must want it with both our thoughts and feelings, and we must also believe that it is possible for us. Many times we desire something with both our thoughts and feelings, but what is missing is the belief that it will show up for us.

"Let's remember that when we place an order through a catalog, we have already mentally accepted the item. We believe we now have it. It's a done deal. We may even have already decided to buy something to go with it, or we may have decided where we'll put it. It's this kind of mental acceptance that is necessary for deliberate creation."

Show the children a mail-order catalog and make sure they understand how the system works. You may even let them place an order to imprint the feeling of mental acceptance.

Suggested Affirmation
I'll see it when I believe it.

18
FOCUS ON THE PICTURE, NOT ON THE FRAME

Materials

A picture in an attractive frame. Place a sheet of paper over the picture.

Lesson

"How silly we would be if we visited an art gallery and concentrated on the frames rather than on the masterpieces within them. That is what we do when we focus on our bodies rather than on the love and spirit that are within them. The masterpiece the Creator has set within the temporary frames of our bodies is what we want to think about. We are much more than our bodies."

Another analogy you may use is that of a space suit. "Just as space suits would be needed if we were to visit another planet, we need to put on a space suit when we come to this planet. It's called a body. Our bodies are not the real us. We existed before being in our bodies, and we'll still exist when we leave our bodies."

The children may act out being visitors in an art gallery admiring frames or being astronauts choosing and putting on space suits. Remind them that they want to look for the Light, or the spiritual qualities, in others and not be caught up in frames or space suits.

Suggested Affirmation
I enjoy looking beyond the body to the inner person.

19
PURE THOUGHTS

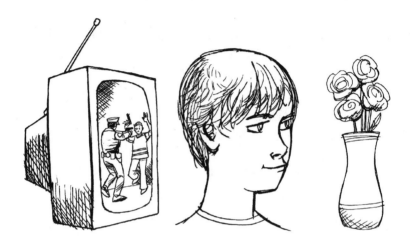

Materials

Masking tape, dark-colored swatches of felt or an old sweater or coat.

Lesson

If we want to be full of Joy and close to Spirit, we need to avoid the low vibrations, such as profanity, pornography, and violence, including simply viewing these things, like on a television program. When our mind is cluttered with such thoughts, it becomes impure. Impurity attracts more impurity.

Wrap masking tape around the children's hands with the sticky side out. Have him/her rub the tape on a dark piece of felt or an old sweater or coat. Point out how the fuzz from the felt or clothing sticks to the tape.

Explain that our minds are like the tape and that they retain what they are exposed to. These impure thoughts stick in the mind and are nearly impossible to remove. Have a child try to remove the pieces of fuzz from the tape.

Suggested Affirmation
I keep my thoughts loving, clean, and pure.

SPROUTS

FOR THE MORE ADVANCED LEARNER

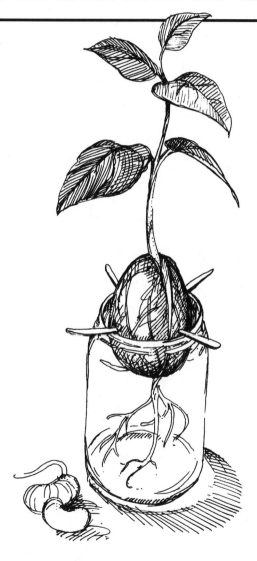

20
LIKE ATTRACTS LIKE

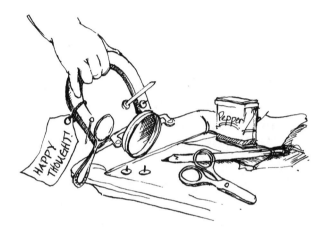

Materials

A strong magnet or two, a washable felt marker, two slips of paper, pieces of tape, and a tray of small objects, some of which contain iron or steel. These small objects can be found quickly in the kitchen or bathroom, such as a paper cup, straw, toothpick, pencil, paper clip, measuring spoon, potato peeler, corkscrew, jar lid, bottle opener, nail, spice can, scissors, egg timer, nutcracker, scouring pad, salt shaker, tweezers, tube of lipstick or lip gloss, small mirror, and so forth. Test the objects beforehand to be sure the magnet will pick up a few of the items, and know which ones they are.

Lesson

You may wish to let the children experiment first to see which items the magnet will attract. If they don't know, point out the common denominator of these objects: iron.

"There is a law that says 'Like attracts like.' It's called the law of attraction, and it's thought to be the most powerful law in the universe. It says that when we have a conscious thought and corresponding feeling, we send energy through our body, and as we send energy through our body, we attract the same energy or vibration from elsewhere.

"Let me show you how it works. We'll pretend that these items are all thoughts, including this magnet. Let's say that this magnet is a happy thought. [Label it *Happy Thought* with a slip of paper.] It thinks, 'I have so many great friends.' Here are two objects. One is a happy thought: 'I'm a good singer' [hold up a magnetic object]; the other is sad: 'I'm awful at sports' [hold up a nonmagnetic object]. Which thought do you think this magnetic thought will attract? [Wait for a response.] Remember, the law is 'Like attracts like.' Sure enough, it attracted the happy thought. Let's see if it happens again. These are the thoughts: 'Teacher likes me,' and 'My brother is mean.' Sure enough, it attracted the positive thought. [Remove objects from the tray as they are used.]

"Now let's take the other magnet [if there are two] [or change the name of the one magnet and label it *Unhappy Thought*]. Maybe it's 'Poor me, nobody likes me.' What kinds of thoughts do you think it will attract? Remember the law. Perhaps nobody will play with you if you focus on that thought. Can you name some unhappy thoughts? Each of those unhappy thoughts will attract another one. [Demonstrate with the magnet and other objects how an unhappy thought will attract more of the same thoughts.]

"People thinking happy thoughts will attract to themselves happy, positive people who are fun to be around. If they keep thinking unhappy thoughts, they will attract other negative people and experiences. The way their energy flows, positive or negative, dictates how they vibrate. They will attract according to their vibration."

Suggested Affirmation
I focus on the positive and attract only good things to myself.

21
THE POWER OF
AFFIRMATIONS

This lesson is best used after Lesson 20,
"Like Attracts Like," and the two parts are best used
at different times.

Materials

Part 1: A clear drinking glass three-quarters full of water, a bottle of food coloring, a spoon, some liquid bleach in a small glass, and an eyedropper (a straw may be used in lieu of the eyedropper).

Part 2: A glass and enough small pebbles or beans to fill the glass.

Lesson

Part 1: Explain that the glass represents a person's mind and the water represents thoughts held in the mind. Point out how this mind is full of clear, clean thoughts. Ask for examples of positive, happy kinds of thoughts that the water might represent. Then let the children put in a drop of food coloring and call it a negative thought. Ask them what this thought might be and have a suggestion yourself, such as "I can't speak in front of other people" or "What dumb ideas I have!" You might say, "Oops! Here comes another negative thought," as you add another drop of food coloring.

Ask the children what could have attracted these thoughts. Help the children remember the "Like attracts like" law, which states that a negative thought will draw to it more negative thoughts.

Repeat the process of adding negativity until the water is fully colored. Then ask the children to think of prevalent negative statements heard at school or on television. Explain that people with minds full of negativity are probably feeling very tired because people burn physical energy three times faster when they are thinking negatively than when they are thinking positively!

Ask the children if they have ideas about how to get rid of all that negativity—all those fear, doubt, and limitation thoughts. Teach them about statements that can work amazingly well for them. (See "Guidelines for Affirmations.") Explain that it often takes many positive thoughts to cancel out a negative thought because the negative thoughts have usually been put in with much more feeling or emotion than the positive ones have.

Let the colored water represent one fear or limitation the children may feel. Make up an affirmation to counteract it, and have them add a drop of bleach to the water. Ask them to repeat this affirmation, or a similar one, while they add more drops of bleach. For example, if they have a fear of being dumb or not as capable as others, the affirmation might be "I am a smart person," "I have lots of ability," or "I am a fast learner." Stir the water now and then to mix in the bleach, and repeat this portion of the lesson until the water is back to its clear, positive condition. (Practice ahead of time so you'll know how much bleach you need to clear the water—about ten to one, just as more positivity is needed to cancel negativity.)

Part 2: For an alternative analogy to show the power of affirmation, use a small glassful of water and enough small pebbles or dried beans to fill the glass. Compare the negativity stored in our minds to the water in the glass, and suggest that the pebbles represent affirmations, which can displace the negativity. Larger pebbles or beans can be used for affirmations put in (stated) with great emotion or feeling. They carry more power because feelings create. Again, one thought can be used, and the pebbles can represent specific affirmations. For instance, if a child feels a lack of friends, the affirmations might be "New friends are continually coming into my life," "I am a warm and loving person," "I am responsive to other people's needs," "I have friends by being one," or "I have an abundance of friends."

Suggested Affirmation
I can choose how I feel by the way I think and talk.

22

THINK ABOUT WHAT YOU WANT, NOT ABOUT WHAT YOU DON'T WANT

Materials

Two drinking glasses about two-thirds full of dirt, a spoon, a bowl, and a sink with running water.

Lesson

"We are the glass, and the dirt represents a negative condition or problem in our lives. We can clean out this problem in two different ways. One way is by digging at the problem and scraping it out, which is what we do when we concentrate hard on the problem by trying to solve it." Scrape the dirt from the glass into a bowl, showing how the glass still isn't very clean.

"The other way is much easier because all we have to do is place the glass with dirt under a water faucet and let the water run on it for about five minutes." Do so.

The water represents the flow of energy, of positive thoughts and mental pictures that concentrate only on the desired result while giving no thought to the problem. Full attention is put on the end result, not on the means of getting the result. These positive thoughts can be visualizations, affirmations, decrees, or calls. This method washes the problem away effortlessly, without struggle. If we need to act, we receive that guidance by listening to our Inner Teacher.

While the glass is becoming clean, or clear of the dirt, name a problem familiar to the children, and ask them for affirmations and mental-picture suggestions that can be used to wash the problem away. Then reverse the process. Display a glass of clear water (representing the children full of positive thoughts) and show how cloudy it can get when even a small amount of negative thinking (dirt) is introduced.

How we flow our energy, that is, the way in which we vibrate, is a major determinant of our life experiences.

Suggested Affirmation
I flow my energy toward what I want, not what I don't want.

23
THE POWER OF LOVE

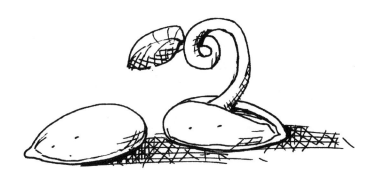

Materials
Two containers for soil or water, and pumpkin seeds.

Lesson
Before planting your seeds, place both containers in similar surroundings, but keep separate from each other.

Container #1: When putting seeds into water or soil, speak kind, loving words, using a gentle voice: "I care for you and you will grow, blossom, and make my heart happy." Continue this process for several days until you see the sprouts.

Container #2: Speak negative words to this seed, using unpleasant expressions and an angry voice: "You will never germinate, but if you do you will be weak, never have blossoms or strong stems." Continue this process for several days. Notice the difference between the plants.

Now, talk about happy and negative surroundings, people, and atmospheres. Discuss how wonderfully we grow when we are appreciated, loved, and cherished, and how hard it is to survive with low self-esteem, poor self-image, or when we are under pressure or are being criticized. Elicit examples and have appropriate stories to share.

Suggested Affirmation
I blossom when I am loved.

24
WHAT GETS MY ATTENTION GETS ME

Materials

A container, such as a bud vase, water bottle, or ketchup bottle, several pieces of string, scissors, and an assortment of objects. Extend the strings from the neck of the vase to the objects. If necessary, use tape to connect them.

Lesson

"The vase [or bottle] represents us, and the strings represent our attention. There is a spiritual law that says, 'What you put your attention on, you connect with, and the essence of it comes back to you through your attention. Where your attention goes, energy flows.'

"So, if your attention settles on something you don't want in your life [run your finger along the string to one object], what you need to do is snip that string. Think of this as a telephone line that can send messages back and forth. If the line is cut, there are no more messages." Snip the string.

Suggest that the objects represent situations that could have gotten our attention in a negative way. Give your own example, such as "I was thinking today about how critical _____ is. It seems as if nothing ever pleases her. She criticizes everything. But if I dwell on the way she criticizes, I'll draw more critical people or critical attitudes to myself. So what I want to do is quickly snip that thread of attention [snip a string] and free myself from that negativity.

"Now, let's have an example of something you may have put your attention on that you wouldn't want in your life." As examples are offered, assign one to each object that has a string attached. Snip the string as the law—"What you put your attention on comes back to you"—is restated.

The children might give examples such as "Daddy not finding a job," "Fighting about television," "Chores I don't like to do," "Someone stealing my bike," "Not having spending money like the other kids," or "Being a slow reader."

"Anytime you're aware that your attention is on something you don't want in your life, you can mentally snip the string and quickly think about what you do want. Our feelings are the key to our attention. They are more powerful than thought. They carry more energy."

Add another object and connect a string to it also. "This represents Spirit. If we contemplate the love, wisdom, and power of Spirit, the same law will attract these qualities to us. What gets our attention gets us, so let's put our attention on the highest thought we know of."

End the lesson by extending strings to several new objects, each representing a positive idea the children would want to keep their attention on, such as friendships, health, good grades, and learning a new skill.

Suggested Affirmation

I keep my attention on the positive and the good.

25
THOUGHTS DON'T LEAVE
THEIR SOURCE

Materials

A pencil and either carbonless paper in duplicate (such as that used in offices for invoices) or two sheets of paper with carbon paper between them for each child and adult.

Lesson

Ask the children to think of happy and unhappy thoughts that they recently have had toward others. Encourage an awareness of both loving, kind thoughts and hateful, angry, resentful thoughts. To aid the memory process, provide some of your real-life examples. With each one you recall, write a word or two describing it on your paper. Have the children do the same, using symbols instead of words if writing doesn't come easily. For instance, a circle could stand for a loving feeling and a scribble for an angry feeling.

After the list is completed, label the top sheet *My Body and Brain* and the bottom one *Other People*. Point out how all our thoughts and feelings leave their marks on our bodies and brains. They don't just leave us and go out to the other person.

Explain, at each child's level, "The vibrations of our emotions affect our bodies, and our thoughts make an impression in our brains, which affects the way we see our world. Therefore, we can never give away hurtful or hateful thoughts. Whatever we're feeling is affecting us more than it is affecting the other person. Sometimes the other person isn't even aware of our feelings. Whatever we give—loving or hurtful—is given to ourselves first, as on the top sheet, and then passed on to the other person." The carbon copy is usually a bit lighter than the top copy. Use this to show that we are more affected by our hurtful remarks or thoughts than the other person is.

"We can help ourselves by thinking happy, kind, loving thoughts because they have a healing and harmonizing effect on our bodies." Ask both children and adults to write some positive thoughts about specific people, and then observe how these emotions were recorded on the "My Body and Brain" sheets first.

Suggested Affirmation
I am careful to think thoughts that help me and others.

26
DO YOUR WORDS HAVE WEIGHTS OR WINGS?

Materials

Two pieces of paper or cardboard folded in half to make stand-up signs (see illustration). Sketch an anchor or another kind of weight on one and wings on the other. Provide a pile of single words cut from newspapers or magazines, or pencils and small scraps of paper, or both.

Lesson

"Sticks and stones may break my bones, but words can never hurt me." Ask the children if they think this old poem is true. Ask for examples of why or why not. Most people agree that our words can lift people up or weigh them down. The same is true of our thoughts because words are just symbols of thoughts.

Work together to come up with commonly used words that help people feel uplifted or weighed down. Write them on slips of paper, and put them by the appropriate sign. Next, look through the pile of words you've clipped out, and place them by the appropriate sign.

"Words that are like weights or anchors make us feel heavy, discouraged, limited, lacking, or fearful in some way. This includes not just put-downs, but negative news, criticism, probing, or anything that creates the illusion of separation among people. Such words are a form of separation because they ignore that the other person is also a child of the Creator.

"Words that help us feel light are sincere words that lift us, that make us feel capable, lovable, and positive. Such words make us feel good about ourselves, others, and the world around us. 'Feel Good' words bring light into our minds and hearts, while 'Feel Bad' words bring darkness." Suggest that the children become careful observers of people's reactions so that they will know how other people are responding to their words.

This lesson focuses on the effect a word or thought has on others. Make sure the children understand that their words can also have a powerful effect on themselves. If they're thinking gloom-and-doom thoughts, being critical of themselves, or speaking of lack or limitation, then they are creating darkness instead of light in their minds. Self-criticism can hurt more than criticism from others because, if it comes from outside us, we always can choose to reject it, but self-criticism is not usually rejected.

End with participants speaking to each other using only words with wings—words that uplift.

Suggested Affirmation
My words have wings; they uplift me and others.

61

27
THE FORMATIVE POWER
OF IMAGINATION

Materials

Scissors and paper for each child and adult.

Lesson

The paper represents the energy or substance of which the universe is made. The scissors represent our imagination.

"Some people say that imagination is like the scissors of the mind. You can use your imagination like scissors to cut anything you choose out of the universal substance." Ask for specific examples of what the children would like, and then ask them to cut symbolic shapes out of the paper. Start by stating your concrete examples: a trip, a certain job or talent, a new home, and so on. Cut symbols of these examples from your paper and label them.

"Our imagination is one of the greatest powers we have and should be used with great care. Whatever we vividly imagine with faith on a repeated basis can come into our lives, so we must imagine only things we want to experience." Give examples of the use of imagination that relate to the children's world at this time: winning a prize, making a friend, being ill, failing a test, losing something, falling while skating, and so on.

Remind them that they have the choice of using their imaginations either constructively or destructively. Discuss how the "muscle" of the imagination needs to be exercised like any other muscle, or it may wither away from lack of use. If time allows, include some creative thinking exercises to further stretch their imaginations. My book *The Joyful Child: A Sourcebook of Activities and Ideas for Releasing Children's Natural Joy* has plenty to choose from. Begin with fanciful "What if" and "Just suppose" questions.

Conclude with a visual-imagery exercise in which the children close their eyes and use their imaginations to construct some good they want in their lives. Here are some suggestions:

- Imagine what a perfect day would be like from start to finish.
- Imagine where you would most want to go if you could take a trip.
- Imagine improvement in academic skills or sports.

Suggested Affirmation
I use my imagination creatively and wisely.

28

OUR INVISIBLE BRIDGE

Materials

A 12-inch ruler and a small cardboard box, like a shoebox, with
an opening of less than 12 inches. The box could be empty or
filled with stones and the like, representing the obstacles or
unknowns of life.

Lesson

Explain that there is an invisible bridge that leads to the "good"
we want. The bridge is made of Love, Joy, and Gratitude. Have
each word on a small piece of paper and have a child tape the
paper firmly onto the ruler, making it into a bridge of Love, Joy,
and Gratitude. This ruler will make a bridge across the box to

the "good" that the children want. Give them time to silently decide what they most want. Sharing is OK as long as you make it optional; it is honoring their privacy and feelings to let children keep their wishes to themselves if they wish.

Explain that the bridge is in our heart. It is made up of three feelings: One, Love for the object or experience; two, the Joy you know you will feel; and three, the Gratitude in your heart. One by one, name the three feelings and give the children time to feel the Love, Joy, and Gratitude.

Affirmation
Love, Joy, and Gratitude lead me to my Good.

29
DELIBERATE CREATION

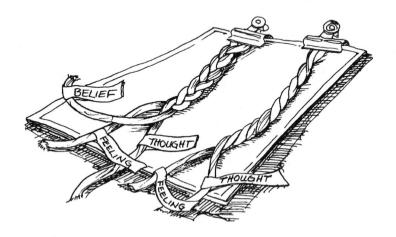

This lesson is presented in two parts. It can be approached in two ways, depending on the children's ages or levels of understanding.

Materials
Part 1: Two strands of different colors of yarn or cord for each child. Tape the strands of yarn or cord down to a flat surface or tie the pieces to something so they can be twisted and braided together.

Part 2: Three strands of yarn or cord (three colors) that are secured with tape or tied down in some way so they can be braided.

Lesson

Part 1: This lesson serves as a quick reminder that our heads and our hearts must be in agreement in order to create whatever we want in our lives.

Give each child two strands of different colors of yarn or cord. Identify one as thought and the other as feeling. Elaborate on the idea that a feeling with a thought creates emotion. It is the feeling that provides the energy to move the thought forward so the thought can become a thing or an experience.

Ask the children to think of something they want, such as an improved skill or a fun experience. Choose a strand to represent this thought, and suggest that the second strand be the feeling, the passion, for this idea. Ask the children to twist the strands tightly together to symbolize how their minds' and their hearts' desires must be fully integrated to get the wanted results. Such emotion is key to co-creation.

Part 2: This exercise presents a more complete picture of deliberate creation because a third strand of yarn is introduced to represent belief or expectancy. We may passionately want something, but unless we believe it is possible for us, it won't become real. In any creation, there is always some balance between belief and desire.

This may be a fun time for a child to learn to braid while repeating a specific thought, feeling, and belief for each strand, such as "I want to learn to swim" (thought), "After all, if other kids swim there is no reason why I can't" (feeling), and "I believe it is possible for me to be a good swimmer" (belief).

You may wish to expand this lesson to explain how true joy results from an alignment of our inner and outer selves, our personality and soul, our head and heart.

Suggested Affirmation

I can bring about good in my life by intertwining my thoughts, feelings, and beliefs.

30
CHANGE IS NEEDED
FOR GROWTH

This lesson is especially useful when a child is facing a change
or a risk, perhaps like joining scouts or a soccer team,
going away to camp, staying overnight with a friend
for the first time, or entering a new school.

Materials

A real houseplant that has become bound by its roots in its
current pot and needs transplanting. If a rootbound plant
is not available, use a tiny clay flowerpot or a small cardboard transplanting pot, a large tangled mass of string stuffed
into the pot, and an artificial flower to be inserted into the
string mass.

Lesson

If you don't use a houseplant, explain that the mass of string represents the roots of the flower. "Roots need a lot of soil to grow in, but these roots have grown so that there is hardly room for any soil. We need to remove the plant from the old pot and put it into a larger one, or the plant will always be limited in size."

Explain that people are just like the plant, and at times we, too, need more room to grow. Compare the pot to the children's old ways of thinking about themselves. The old pot, or the old ways, can be so comfortable that sometimes we need to push ourselves out of our "comfort zone." If not, our growth will become stunted, just as the plant's growth is stunted when it's in a container that's too small for it. The old pot met the needs of the plant at one time and was good for the plant. Now that the plant has grown, a change is necessary so it can continue its growth.

Discuss how, in order to grow and become all that they can be, children must change their old ideas about themselves. Help them see change as a means of "becoming," and use examples like an acorn breaking apart to sprout a new tree or a caterpillar becoming a butterfly.

Suggested Affirmation

I welcome change in my life because it helps me grow.

31
THERE IS NO SEPARATION

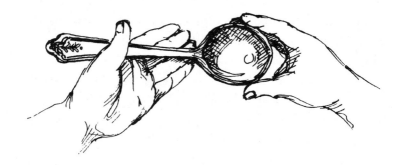

Materials

A silver or stainless-steel teaspoon.

Lesson

Compare the teaspoon to us and the metal used to make the spoon to Spirit.

"If we were to take all the metal out of this spoon, there would no longer be a spoon. There is no way we can separate the metal from the spoon and still have the spoon.

"Now let's say that this spoon is like you and the metal in it is like Spirit. There is no way you can be separated from Spirit because Spirit is in you just as the metal is in the spoon. Spirit is a special love energy that is in everybody and everything. Nothing is separate from Spirit."

Explain at the children's level of understanding:

"The attributes of Spirit—love, peace, order, wisdom, understanding, and so forth—are within us all. We can call on these powers and activate them in our lives. Even though we all have these qualities, they need to be affirmed and called forth." Use a particular example, depending on the needs of the children. For instance, if order is a need in their lives, remind them that they have order in them because it is an attribute of Spirit, and Spirit is in them. They can remind themselves by saying, "I am one with divine order."

Suggest that they play a little mind game: every time they see a teaspoon, they think about Spirit being in them just like the metal is in the spoon.

Suggested Affirmation
I am one with Spirit, or God.

32
OUR CONNECTION WITH THE CREATOR AND WITH EACH OTHER

Materials

An apple cutter. If this is not available, a picture or sketch of a bicycle wheel will do nicely. (An apple is not needed.)

Lesson

The wheel shape, as illustrated by the apple cutter, graphically shows our connection with each other and with the Creator.

"The hub of the wheel [or the center of the apple cutter] represents the Creator. We are the spokes. The closer we get to the Creator, the closer we get to one another. This works the other way around too, because as we get closer to one another, we get closer to God.

"When we're feeling really loving toward someone, we are kind, generous, and thoughtful. We are expressing spiritual qualities. When we are angry and hateful toward someone, we put ourselves farther away from an awareness of the Creator. We can see [point to the outside edge of the cutter] that the farther we are from one another, the farther we are from exhibiting the loving attributes of the Creator."

Ask for examples of how people separate themselves from one another, such as blaming, name-calling, and deceiving. "That is why forgiveness is such an important step in healing our relationships. Such feelings separate us from others and, therefore, from the Creator, who is total, unconditional love. In fact, many people think that the only problem that exists is separation.

"The more we work to express all the qualities that are spiritual, such as peace, love, harmony, and order, the closer we'll feel to other people. Other people will feel these qualities and will want to be closer to us. Together we will move closer to complete spiritual awareness." Encourage a discussion of the ways we can express spiritual qualities in our everyday lives. Start with an example from your own life.

Suggested Affirmation
The closer I grow to people, the closer I feel to the Spirit within me.

33
YOU CAN'T GIVE LOVE
UNLESS YOU HAVE LOVE

Materials

A turkey baster, a bowl of water, and an empty bowl. Optional: Drop red food coloring into the water to make it pink—a color representing love.

Lesson

"The turkey baster represents us—our hearts and minds. The water represents perfect love, which is unconditional acceptance and the absence of all negative emotions. To be filled with perfect love, we need to first empty ourselves of all feelings or emotions that keep us from accepting love. We cannot fully accept love when we feel unworthy or undeserving. Some emotions that make us feel undeserving are guilt, anger, jealousy, and resentment. These can fill us and keep perfect love out of our awareness."

Discuss these kinds of emotions and the concept of low self-esteem at the children's level of understanding. They know what makes them feel unworthy of an abundance of love. "These emotions are all up in the top of the baster, and the baster must be squeezed empty before the water, or pure love, can come in." Discuss ways they might change feelings of unworthiness, irritation, selfishness, and other emotions that are unlike love.

Have the children symbolically blow out negativity while they squeeze the bulb. Give each a turn to hold the squeezed bulb while you guide the baster into the bowl of water (perfect love). Show them that, as they release the bulb, love (the water) fills the baster up. Let the children experiment so they see that, if the negativity hadn't been squeezed out, love couldn't come in.

If the children are old enough, take the lesson to the next step and teach that we can love others only as much as we love ourselves. It is love of self that can motivate us to clean out the bulb of negativity. The empty bowl represents all others. Ask them to share the baster full of love with others by emptying it into the bowl. How much they have to share depends on how full they (the baster) are with love.

Affirmations are a great way to replace negative thought patterns with positive ones and to build self-esteem. Help the children create some to suit their needs.

Suggested Affirmation
I am filled with love for myself and others.

34
LISTENING FOR GUIDANCE

Materials

A large bowl of water and a wooden spoon (or any large spoon). Optional: a picture of a scene reflected in water. Or, if possible, take the children to a lake or pond.

Lesson

Begin by discussing how it is possible to look into a quiet pool and see the reflection of a tree growing on its bank. But if the water is rough or churning, we lose the image. Encourage the children to remember such a scene as you discuss the lesson.

Pretend that the bowl is the pool and the spoon (held vertically) is the tree. As you swish the water with your fingers, explain that if the wind were blowing the water or if children were splashing in it, we would be unable to see the tree's reflection. Explain at their level of understanding: "We each have a guidance factor within us. Some call it the Inner Teacher. It tries to speak to us and give us direction, but it can be heard only if our minds are calm and still like a very quiet pool. The beauty of the tree is not seen in churning water, and the guidance factor is not heard by a churning mind. An overly busy mind focuses on problems. But when the mind is made very quiet, these problems are usually answered. A quiet mind can see beyond confusion to a solution."

Suggest that the children frequently practice stilling their minds so they can listen to that still, small voice of Spirit. You could suggest meditation techniques, such as holding a word like peace or love in their minds, staring at an object, or making a steady humming sound. There are many, many more.

As is possible with many of these lessons, role-playing could enhance your teaching. One child might whisper a message, such as "Call home right away" while another child busy with noisy thoughts (churning the water) is not able to hear it.

Suggested Affirmation
I still my mind and listen within for guidance.

35
BALANCING OUR LIFE

Materials

Glass jar (lid optional) for adult and each child if there are only three or four children. A box or bowl of small, medium, and large rocks. If you have more than three children, you may choose to demonstrate with your jar.

Lesson

The jar represents our day—the time in our day. (It can also be adapted for a week.) The stones or rocks are the activities that we want to get into our day. The bigger rocks represent the longer and more important activities in our day, such as going to school.

Ask what some of the more important things they do in the day are. Start with yourself and name the rocks/stones accordingly (for example, go to work, buy food, cook the food, wash the clothes, wash the dishes, answer telephone calls, do the laundry, and so on).

Now try to get stones in the jar. "Oops; all the rocks won't fit in. What can we learn from this? How can we get all our activities into our day? It looks like we'll have to prioritize and put only the most important one in first.

"Would you agree we need to put in the most important first? [Wait for answer.] That means we put our jobs in first— school for you and the office for me. Since that is the most time, we need to use the biggest rock. What is something else that takes up time? [Wait for their answers. Some suggestions from you might be transportation, preparing meals, eating meals, cleaning up dishes, or cleaning up the house.]

"Now the jar is almost full, so we have to be careful what we plan for one day because we might run out of time for the things we value most."

Some lessons, like this one, may need to be visited more often.

Suggested Affirmation
In the quiet, I listen to the God in me for what is most important each day.

36
THOUGHTS ARE GIFTS

Materials
A small box wrapped like a gift, and several small pieces of paper.

Lesson
Begin by explaining that the gift box doesn't really have a gift in it, but is a symbol of many gifts we receive each day.

"For something to be a gift, does it have to be put in a box and have a ribbon around it? Does it have to be something that is bought? What are some gifts you like to receive that are not bought or wrapped?" Offer ideas such as a warm smile, a special favor, help when stuck or in a hurry, a hug or pat on the back, an invitation, praise or appreciation, a promise to be taken somewhere special, someone to listen when we have a problem, and prayers or loving thoughts sent our way.

"Do you see that each day you receive more gifts than you are aware of? How many do you think you receive each day? Well, I have a big surprise for you. In truth, you are receiving thousands and thousands of gifts each day. You may not think you know about these gifts, but another part of your mind knows. How is this possible?

"There is only One Mind on which each person draws, and we're all part of it. That is why we say that we are all brothers and sisters. Because there is only One Mind, the mind of Spirit, we are truly connected at some level with everyone on the planet. Each day, thousands of people give gifts to each other, and these gifts bless everyone. The more thoughts and acts of joy and happiness in the world, the more joy we'll feel because of our connection with everyone else."

Elaborate on the unity of humanity at the children's levels of awareness. If time allows, include a meditation with a visualization of all the world's people joyfully giving various kinds of gifts.

You may want to expand the lesson with the following: "You, in turn, are giving gifts to brothers and sisters around the world when you befriend or help others or think loving thoughts. Each time you give any sort of gift, you are blessing multitudes of others." On the slips of paper, ask children to write "thought gifts" that they would like to send. Place them in the box. These can be reread or added to when there is a special need.

Suggested Affirmation
Today I rejoice because of the many gifts I give and receive.

81

37
OUR ICEBERGS

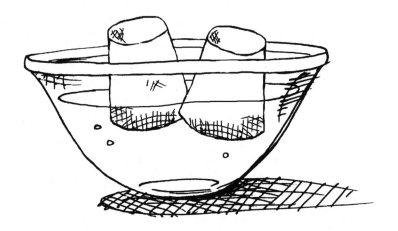

Materials

Small paper cups (for making miniature icebergs), a deep, wide, clear glass bowl, filled with water. Optional: Add blue food coloring to the water to make it more opaque.

Lesson

Before the lesson, make two or three miniature icebergs by filling small paper cups with water and freezing them solid in the freezer. Then run warm water over the outside until the ice slips out or you can tear off the paper cup. Put the ice from the cups into the clear bowl filled with cold water. Notice that most of the ice is below the surface and not very visible. Explain that this is why ships sometimes run into icebergs and get damaged.

There is a part of us that is not visible to others too. Our icebergs are the hidden emotions that we and others forget about until we bump into them. Our parents, schoolmates, neighbors, and even good friends may not see the submerged part of our emotions. The hidden fears and anger that we forget we even have till someone bumps into them. Nor can we see the invisible parts of our friends, neighbors, or schoolmates. That is why we can't fairly criticize them. The Native Americans have a saying; "You can't judge anyone until you have walked a mile in their shoes." We don't know what personal battles each person is facing.

Also, our negative emotions, like hate, anger, and fear, can be as dangerous to people as an iceberg in the ocean is to a ship. They can destroy one's self-esteem and hurt others.

Suggested Affirmation
I won't judge anyone until I have walked in their shoes.

38
DEATH AND THE BODY

Materials

An electric fan (table model), an onion, an ear of corn, and a glove.

Lesson

Some children are confused by death, even though they innately know that the person who died isn't really dead but is very much alive in another dimension. Many younger children can see into that dimension, but for those who can't, some visual analogies may be appropriate.

The shedding of the physical body can be compared to the shedding of the outer skin of an onion or the husk of an ear of corn. Encourage the children to husk the corn or to peel some layers off the onion while you discuss that the inside of the onion or corn can be compared to our spiritual body. "When we look with spiritual eyes, what we see looks just as real as our physical bodies do."

To help the children better understand why we can't see the spiritual body, show them the fan. Show how they can see the blades when the fan is off or in slow motion, but when the fan is on high, the blades are invisible. Compare it to the higher vibration of the invisible dimensions.

Another way to demonstrate the physical-body/spiritual-body relationship is to put a glove on your hand and then peel it off to symbolize the death of the body. Explain that we are clothed with physical matter just like the hand is covered by the glove. You might create a puppet skit in which the hand drops the body (the puppet), but the hand is still very much alive and carries on the conversation.

Suggested Affirmation
I am much more than this body.

FULL BLOOM

FOR THE EXPERIENCED LEARNER

39
ONLY OUR THOUGHTS
HURT US

Materials

Three small boxes about the same size, pencils, and small pieces of paper for each child. Tape pieces of paper with the word *Experience* on the side of one box, the word *Unhappiness* on one side with *Happiness* on the reverse side of another box, and the words *Our Thoughts* on the third box. Arrange the boxes as shown in the illustration.

Lesson

Begin by asking the children to think of an unhappy feeling they've felt recently, such as anger, sadness, jealousy, or resentment. If they are old enough, have them write the word that best expresses their unhappy feeling on a piece of paper and put it into the box labeled *Unhappiness.*

Next, ask them to write on another slip of paper the experience or condition they think made them feel bad. Encourage concise statements, such as "Friend got invited and I didn't," "Fell off my bike," "Dad wouldn't let me watch favorite program," "Lost my cat," or "Sister scribbled on my homework assignment." Put these slips into the box labeled *Experience.*

Now point out that between the two boxes is a box labeled *Our Thoughts.* If the children are aware enough, ask questions regarding what they think must always intercede between an experience and unhappiness.

Explain, in your own way, that the experience never creates the unhappiness. "Unhappiness comes from our thoughts about the experience. Another person can have the same experience and not feel pain, anger, or sadness. We have a choice to feel bad or to feel good, depending on the thoughts we choose to think. So, with the help of our Inner Teacher, we can learn to choose thoughts that bring happiness. [Turn the third box to the word *Happiness.*] We can have whichever one we really want, happiness or unhappiness, by learning to choose our thoughts. Our Inner Teacher can help us if we go quietly within and ask."

Some children may share their painful experiences. Use these for group exploration regarding how a different mode of thinking would lessen the pain. If there are no volunteers, have examples that are at their level of understanding.

Remind them that there is always someone somewhere who would not see the experience or condition as a reason to be unhappy. Our thinking creates our happiness. There are many stories of people in prisoner-of-war camps and other similar places who have discovered this principle.

A guided meditation may be an appropriate way to end the lesson. Have the children ask for spiritual help in looking at a particular experience or problem in a new way. Allow plenty of time for listening.

Suggested Affirmation

I go within and recognize the good in each experience.

40
MY THOUGHTS
JOIN ALL OTHERS

Materials

A strainer, a large bowl, a spoon, and some flour and cinnamon (or instant tea).

Lesson

The bowl stands for the thought world—the atmosphere of everyone's thoughts—that surrounds us all, the strainer represents each person's mind, and the flour and cinnamon represent our thoughts.

Ask for a happy or loving thought from one child, and ask him or her to put a spoonful of flour (representing that thought) into the strainer. Shake the strainer (the child may enjoy doing this), and watch how the happy thought "leaves the mind and spreads into the world of thought—into the universal mind." Explain how all minds are joined in the thought atmosphere, so we are not alone in experiencing the effects of our thinking. Everyone feels a little happier because of the joyful thought that just went out.

"Let's see what would happen if one of you put an unhappy or fearful thought into your mind." Invite another child to share such a thought while he or she drops a spoonful of cinnamon into the strainer and shakes it. "As the thought is stirred into the universal mind, watch how it permeates the thought atmosphere as effectively as the happy thought did. Do you think that some people might choose to be a bit more unhappy because of that thought?"

If the children are old enough, discuss how, because minds are joined, we sometimes tune in to others' thoughts and they tune in to ours. They may have examples of when they knew what someone was going to say or do beforehand or of when others tuned in to what they were thinking.

You could extend the conversation to "mass consciousness" (concepts accepted by most of humanity that limit spiritual realization) and how it can affect us even though we're not aware of it. Examples of mass thinking could be offered while spoonfuls of flour or cinnamon go into the strainer. The television, radio, and newspapers are often sources of group thinking. Here are some examples perpetuated by television:

- Material things will make us happy.
- Women are incompetent and inferior to men.
- Violence is commonplace.
- Drinking is fun.
- Grown-ups are idiots.
- Money solves all problems.
- Authorities are your enemy.

- Revenge is sweet.
- Work is a burden.

Be sure to talk about how we can choose our experiences. We do not need to be victims of the world's thinking. Just because everyone says that it's flu season doesn't mean we have to catch the flu.

Suggested Affirmation

My thoughts affect the entire world.

41
MY WORLD REFLECTS WHAT I PUT INTO IT

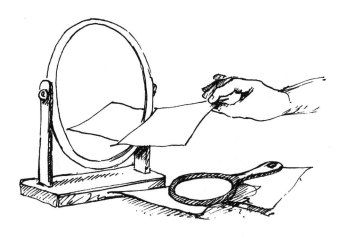

Materials

A small freestanding mirror, a hand or purse mirror for each child (optional), a washable felt marker, a cup, one piece of dark-colored paper and bright-colored paper (one per child is optional), a teaspoon or similar-sized object, and a paper clip.

Lesson

Ask the children to play with the mirror and see how it reflects whatever object it is pointed toward. Show how accurately it displays whatever is reflected into it. "There is a spiritual law—the law of reflection—that works in the same way and does exactly as the mirror does. The mirror represents our world. The world picks up and reflects to us our states of mind, which are our moods and thoughts. We could say that we live in a world of mirrors and that all we see is ourselves. The 'us' we often see is what we focus a lot of energy and judgment on. And what we focus on expands in our lives.

"The mirror of our world is called the 'effect' and our states of mind are called the 'cause of that effect.'" With the marker, write *Effect* on the mirror. Direct the mirror at a spoon so the children see two spoons. "Which spoon is real—the one on the table or the one in the mirror? Just as the one in the mirror is only a reflection, all of life is simply a reflection of what is placed in front of it, a reflection of our consciousness.

"If our minds are full of love, peace, and abundance, the mirror of life will reflect those concepts into our world. If our minds are full of fear, doubt, or anger, the mirror of life will reflect those concepts into our world. An angry person or a fearful situation could come into our lives. If we're feeling sorry for ourselves, the mirror—life—will reflect more experiences to help us feel even sorrier for ourselves.

"At any time, we can withdraw an old thought image and place a new one in front of our mirrors to bring us more happiness." Put the dark-colored paper in front of the mirror to indicate a negative thought. Then pull it away and substitute the bright-colored paper to indicate a positive thought. Ask the children to suggest some thoughts and feelings that the bright paper could represent.

Show what happens if we only partially withdraw the unhappy thoughts and only halfway form new happy ones. Reflect in the mirror half dark paper and half bright paper. Explain that our experiences in life likewise will be a combination of the positive and the negative.

Another idea to illustrate with the mirror is that it can reflect large images just as easily as it does small images. Place a small item, such as a paper clip, in front of the mirror, and then a larger item, such as a cup. Apply this as you see fit to areas in which the children might need to enlarge their thoughts and stop limiting themselves. "The mirror, or our world, can reflect big dreams and goals as easily as small ones because it simply reflects our consciousness. It shows us where we are at that moment in time. If we don't think big, we can't expect big things to come to us." Encourage the children to think their biggest thoughts and then to think a little bigger.

Close the lesson by helping the children see that all of us need to put into our minds only the best, kindest, and most unlimited thoughts, because that is what will be reflected to us. Affirmations can help us do this.

Suggested Affirmation
I look for the good in all things and for the best in all people.

42
WE ABSORB OUR ENVIRONMENT

This lesson may be divided into two parts,
and each part may be enlarged upon.

Materials

Part 1: Pictures clipped from magazines, calendars, newspapers, and so forth, showing a variety of both negative and positive concepts, such as beautiful scenery, happy people, nourishing food, war scenes, accidents, and people drinking and smoking.

Part 2: Two dishes, one with dirty-looking dark water and one with clean, clear water, and two sponges that will fit in the dishes.

Lesson

Part 1: Spread the pictures so the children can see them easily. "There is a law of life that says when we look at a picture of a thing, we are in touch with the spirit of that thing. As we view a picture frequently, we absorb some of the qualities it contains."

Show, one at a time, the positive, beneficial pictures and ask the children to name some of the qualities they would like to absorb or experience. Next, show the negative pictures and talk about the qualities they contain that would be harmful to absorb.

Expand the conversation to include all the pictures children view frequently: television, movies, pictures at home and at school, magazines, billboards, pictures on buses, and so on. Discuss the effect these pictures would have if they were viewed regularly and their qualities were absorbed. Explain that these pictures are a part of their environment, their physical surroundings.

Part 2: Point out the two dishes of water and explain that one represents an environment of negative influences, the other an environment that is positive and uplifting. Then place one sponge in each dish. "The sponge is like a person. Watch it absorb its environment. We tend to absorb much that goes on around us, which is why those who care about us don't want us in certain settings, around certain people, or watching certain television shows and movies.

"A sponge full of dirty water, or negative influences, will have no room left for the pure, clean water, or positive influences. Some of the dirty water will have to be squeezed out to make room for the new water. [Demonstrate.] The same is true with us.

"For instance, if we have friends who encourage us to do things we know are not right, we may have to eliminate them from our lives to make room for more beneficial friendships. Or if we spend time watching television shows that don't contain qualities we really want in our lives, we need to eliminate them so we have more time to soak up qualities or ideas we do desire." Choose examples that the children can relate to while emphasizing these two points: One, we tend to absorb those qualities prevalent in our environment; two, the negative often has to be eliminated to make room for the positive.

A guided meditation could follow in which the children realize what would be beneficial to add to or eliminate from their environments.

Suggested Affirmation
I release what is not for my best, and I choose a positive, uplifting environment.

43
TAKE TIME TO RELAX

Materials

An average-sized rubber band, one colored rubber band for each child, a box or book that the rubber band will barely stretch around, and a small paper wad.

Lesson

Pull the rubber band to show how much stretch there is in it, and then put it around the large box or book. "Rubber bands are made to stretch to fit around bigger items, and hold things together. But what might happen if the rubber band is stretched out for very long? If a rubber band is kept under tension, if it is stretched out all the time, it will deteriorate rapidly and break.

We must allow it to return to its natural state [remove the band from the box] in order for it to last a long time.

"People are very much like the rubber band. They also need to relax or they won't function as well as they are designed to function. Some say that when things get tight, something's got to give. When people are under tension or strain, two areas that often give way are their health and their relationships." Perhaps you have other examples, such as schoolwork or piano practice.

Someone once said that real maturity is not growing up so much as it is growing in. Explain to the children that they have an Inner Teacher who can help them with their challenges if they take some time each day to relax and listen within.

Demonstrate with a paper wad that, the farther back we pull the rubber band, the farther forward it will shoot something. Remind the children that the deeper we go into our inner world, the more effective we can be in the outer world. In silence, we draw back into a knowingness of our true identity. Great works require much time in the silence. Gandhi did "silent sitting" one full day every week.

Discuss what time of day would be best for the children to be alone, to relax with closed eyes, and to listen within. Generally, the amount of time should be one minute for each year of age.

Give each child a colored rubber band as a reminder to have silent sitting time each day.

This lesson could be especially valuable for overly active children. It could also be slanted to help the children better understand why adults need their own quiet time.

You may wish to take an extra few minutes and have the children do a relaxation exercise. The simplest is to have them close their eyes, take three or four really deep breaths, and then think about a happy experience. Another simple but effective technique is to have them get in a very relaxed position, close their eyes, and concentrate on their breathing while they breathe through their noses. Several books are available with centering and meditation exercises for children. My book, The *Joyful Child*, includes a chapter of such exercises.

Suggested Affirmation
I take time each day to relax and to listen within.

44
CHOOSE YOUR THOUGHTS

Materials

Several typical kitchen items that present choices. Here are some examples:

- Two packages or cans of soup
- Two sizes of pots and a package of rice
- A pudding box and a gelatin-dessert box
- Two grocery-store ads
- Two or three similar recipes

Lesson

"These items represent some of the constant choices I make in the kitchen: which recipe is best, which soup to make for dinner, which size pot to use to fit the package of rice, which brand or type of item is the best buy at the store, and so on." Demonstrate how you make some correct choices, perhaps showing which pot fits the quantity of rice.

"We are continually making choices throughout our days, though we may not be aware that we are. We are constantly choosing thoughts and feelings. We are reaching out with loving thoughts, or we are withdrawing with fear, because love and fear are the two basic emotions from which all others stem. One brings us joy, the other pain. All day long, we have the opportunity to choose the thoughts that can either hurt or help us. But when we're feeling anger, hurt, jealousy, irritation, or self-pity, we can remind ourselves that underneath these feelings, it is really fear we are feeling.

"The law of attraction says we attract that which we think about, so we want to be sure that we choose love thoughts, not fear thoughts. Love thoughts are healing and helpful, and they certainly bring more joy into our lives."

If the children are old enough, teach that fear can arrive if one has a false belief in a power other than God. Because there is only one power, God, there is nothing to fear.

Throughout the day, we adults need to keep asking ourselves if we are acting out of love or out of fear. Remember that we teach what we are, or as the old saying goes, "More is caught than taught."

Suggested Affirmation
I let go of fear and choose only loving thoughts.

45
IMPORTANCE OF "OUR OWN CLIMATE"

Materials

Two pots of blossoming "Morning Glory" and a big box. Locate a dark space, such as the box or a closet in the room, and a sunny place, such as a window or under a lamp.

Lesson

Keep both plants in the dark room for thirty minutes. "Notice that the blossoms are closed." Now place them either under the light or on the sunny window ledge for thirty minutes. "Notice how the blossoms are opening. When we are in stress, isolated from the outside world, and with low awareness, our lives are shrinking. When we are open, nurtured, and looking for the best, we grow physically, emotionally, and spiritually."

Suggested Affirmation
My spirit opens up to the light of the Creator, just as flowers open up to the sun.

46
THINGS TAKE FORM
ACCORDING TO OUR
THOUGHTS

Materials

Baker's clay (recipe follows) is suggested, but you can use bread dough, cookie dough, play dough, or natural clay.

Baker's clay recipe:
4 cups flour
1 cup salt
1½ cups water

Mix ingredients and knead with your hands for about five minutes. Give each child a chunk the size of a small grapefruit. This inedible dough is popular for Christmas-tree ornaments, jewelry, and figurines. Objects can be dried at room temperature or baked on a cookie sheet in a 350-degree oven for about forty to sixty minutes. They are done when they have turned light brown or when a toothpick inserted in the thickest part comes out clean, showing that the dough has hardened.

Lesson

Let the children play with the dough in their own way for a bit, and then suggest that it could symbolize the invisible substance or energy of which all things are made. Because thought molds substance into form, suggest that they think of their hands as thoughts. You might even print *Thoughts* on their hands with a washable felt marker. Have them squeeze, poke, and pull at the dough while they think, My *thoughts are molding this substance.* Tell them that this is how thoughts become things: by people thinking about those things.

If you are working with older children, you could expand the lesson and explain that it is really thoughts empowered by feelings that become things. "Idle thoughts have little power, but when a feeling is attached to a thought, we have emotion. Emotional energy is necessary to bring thoughts into visible, physical reality. The invisible substance is immensely sensitive to our thoughts and feelings, and it can be molded easily by them."

Next, have the children form the dough into objects to use as a reminder of the lesson. "What are some of the thoughts you want to mold into form?" Sometimes the things we want to give form to are not easy to make with our hands, so we use symbols. "What could we make to symbolize joy, peace, or love?"

If they choose to make ornaments to hang, insert a paper clip into the top before drying or baking the ornament. Completed objects may be kept natural or may be decorated with felt-tip pens, enamel, watercolor, food dye, or a mixture of equal parts of tempera and white glue.

Suggested Affirmation

I watch my thoughts because thoughts with feelings become things.

47
THERE IS A GIFT IN EVERY PROBLEM

Materials

Several sheets of scratch paper and a pencil, a small wastebasket about half-full of crumpled newspaper, and a tiny gift box with a bow on it under the newspaper. Inside the gift box, put slips of paper with messages at the children's level of understanding. Here are some suggestions:

- My problems help me to grow.
- Problems are friends because they help me become strong.
- There is a lesson in this challenge, and we are never presented with lessons until we are ready to learn from them.
- Something good will come from this problem.

- Within every disadvantage there is an advantage. I look for it now.
- My problems are learning opportunities.
- There is a solution to every problem.
- What is the gift from this experience?
- Failure is positive feedback.
- Problems are guidelines, not stop signs.
- Problems make life more interesting.

Lesson

Ask the children to name some problems in their lives now. Suggest that they include anxieties about future problems that may be of concern, including some local, national, and international problems. As each is named, write it on a piece of scratch paper and invite the children to crumple it and toss it into the wastebasket. (Older children may write down the problems themselves.)

After all the problems are in the wastebasket, explain that there is always a gift hidden within any problem or misfortune, but we need to look for it. Hand the wastebasket to a child and ask the child to look within the midst of the problems for the hidden gift.

Have the child open the gift box, and together read the slips of paper inside. Encourage discussion of these concepts and be prepared with some examples from your experience to illustrate them.

Suggest that when they find the gift in a problem, it will help them if they rename the problem. Call problems "challenges," "learning opportunities," or "growth gifts."

The children might like to have similar gift boxes in their rooms as reminders of the lesson.

Suggested Affirmation

There is good for me in every situation. (You may prefer to use one of the affirmations from the gift list at the beginning of this lesson.)

48

ARE YOU GOING
AROUND IN CIRCLES?

Materials

A terra cotta garden pot and lumps of play dough (used to represent the caterpillars).

Lesson

On our Life Path we need to welcome change and opportunity, or we may become like the processionary caterpillars that Jean Henri Fabre, the great French naturalist, studied. These caterpillars feed on pine needles, and they move through the trees in a long procession, one leading and the others following with their heads snugly fitted against the rears of their predecessors.

Fabre experimented with them and put them on the rim of a large flowerpot. He got the first one connected with the last one and round and round they went. Through sheer force of habit, the creeping circle kept moving around the flowerpot for seven days and nights. Food was in sight and nearby but they continued on the beaten path, until Fabre stopped them.

"Where in your life are you following others' habits or customs blindly?" Discuss. "Are you mistaking activity for accomplishment?"

Suggested Affirmation

I am aware when I mistake activity for accomplishment.

49
RISE ABOVE THE PROBLEM

Materials

Yarn or string. If you will only be demonstrating, have eight pieces, each about two or three feet long. If the children will participate, have similar lengths for each child. Optional mobile project: waxed paper, liquid starch for dipping the yarn, and two wire coat hangers per child.

Lesson

It has been said that we should not try to solve a problem at the level of the problem. We need to rise above the problem and see it as the Creator sees it, which is not to see a problem at all. Our problems are best solved from a spiritual perspective, not by mental power.

Begin with one length of yarn, and thoroughly knot and tangle it so well that it would be extremely difficult to unravel. If the children are participating, invite them to do the same with their yarn.

"This mess represents our human problems, the messes we sometimes find ourselves in. In our minds, we might wrestle with these problems and try to untangle them, but usually a mental approach is long, frustrating, difficult, and not very effective. How easy do you think it would be to untangle and unknot your piece of yarn? It would be like trying to solve a problem all by yourselves. You might miss a knot here and there, and so you might come up with a solution that is not the very best.

"But if you turn the problem over to a higher power, it will be solved in the best way possible. The Creator rises above the mess and doesn't get caught up in it. In fact, the Creator does not see our problems, only our perfection.

"Let's say that this tangled mess represents a relationship problem. Some classmates are difficult to get along with. They're always giving you a bad time. But where you see disharmony, the Creator sees only harmony."

Take another strand of yarn and make a harmonious design. Invite the children to do the same if they are participating.

"This is how God would see that relationship. If you can learn to see as the Creator sees, you will see all of your relationships as loving and harmonious, and you will not have a tangled mess in your life like the knotted yarn. [Toss the tangled yarn aside.]

"Now let's make another knotty problem. [Knot and tangle another piece of yarn.] This is a health problem that we're having or that someone we know is having. But we must remember that the Creator sees us all as whole and healthy, like this. [Shape another piece of yarn, and invite the children to do the same.] The more we can raise ourselves above the thoughts of illness and see ourselves and others as the Creator sees us, the more healthy we'll all be.

"Let's say we are experiencing disorder and confusion in our lives. [Tangle another piece of yarn.] By rising above the problem and seeing it from the spiritual viewpoint, we would see that only divine order exists. [Make a pleasing, orderly shape.] When we choose to see perfect order, we draw that to us.

"Or maybe we're seeing ourselves as so limited in our abilities that we think we are not able to do things as well as other  people do. Again, we need to get way above that man-made problem and see ourselves as the Creator does, as having unlimited ability because of the Spirit within us. [Again, shape a strand of yarn in an orderly design.]

"The next time you have a problem, instead of using human effort, ask Spirit to work out the perfect solution. The universe always works things out in the way that is best for you and for everybody else too. You can have astounding results beyond those that your human mind can imagine or accomplish, but you must sincerely ask.

"After you have asked, you must take time to listen to Spirit within so you will know what your part in the solution is. You must follow up based on the guidance or impression you get. Spirit works through us. Prayer plus action is the formula."

As a reminder of this lesson, consider making mobiles. The lengths of yarn can be dipped in starch and shaped on waxed paper. Make some shapes into the tangled messes to represent problems, and make other designs to represent the way the Creator sees us: healthy, orderly, harmonious, talented, and so forth. After the shapes dry overnight, remove them from the waxed paper and hang them from coat hangers or bent wires to form mobiles.

Suggested Affirmation
I turn my problems over to the Creator and do what I am guided to do.

50
USING OUR DAILY ENERGY

Materials

A glass jar about one pint in size, enough large marbles to fill it, a glass of muddy-colored water, and a flashlight. If marbles are not available, try walnuts in the shell or large stones. Optional: a kitchen timer.

Lesson

"The jar represents the body—yours or anybody's. Within our bodies are many atoms. These marbles represent the atoms that make up the cells of our bodies. They are very far apart in our bodies, but because they are constantly moving, they make our bodies look and feel solid. But there's really a lot of empty space in our bodies and in all objects, such as tables and chairs." Point to the table, chairs, and other objects, and discuss the fact that there is empty space in them.

Next take the flashlight and shine light down over the jar (the body). "The light represents the portion of energy received each day from the Universe. We constantly make choices, minute by minute, as to how we use that energy. Whenever we think unhappy or unloving thoughts, the energy is colored or qualified by that thinking.

"When we think as Spirit would have us think—positively, constructively, without limits—our energy is permeated with this feeling. That energy goes forth and is used for good.

"But what about the energy that is negative? The negativity has made it dark and heavy. Let's say that this glass of muddy-looking water is the light or energy we have misused. We may have used it for anger, judgment, criticism, jealousy, worry, self-pity, or selfishness." Ask the children for examples of the ways they have misused their energy.

Pour the water into the jar. "Because the muddy water is too impure to be used for good, it stays in all the empty spaces in our bodies. Then we may feel heavy and dense because, normally, there is light among all our atoms." Shine the flashlight on the marbles again. Older children may have examples of when they've felt heavy and when they've felt light.

"Our negative thoughts and feelings cut out a lot of the light and actually block the flow of energy in our bodies. This can lead to disease, so we need to become very aware of our thoughts and feelings and quickly change the negative ones. One way to do this is to use a kitchen timer. Carry it around the house and continually set it for ten to twenty minutes. Each time it rings, check your thinking and feeling to see how your daily gift of energy is being used. The more energy we're able to use positively, the more we're masters of ourselves."

If the question comes up about getting rid of the muddy-looking stuff around the marbles, suggest that the children might forgive themselves for misusing their energy, and understand that they did the best their awareness permitted at the time.

In addition, they could start visualizing clear white light beaming through every part of their bodies. This can be done as a guided visualization exercise to end the lesson.

Suggested Affirmation

I think, feel, see, hear, and speak only loving thoughts.

51
THE ASPECTS
OF THE MIND

Materials

A kitchen funnel. Put a strip of non-transparent tape around the funnel just above the stem, as shown in the illustration above. As an alternative, shape heavy paper to represent the cone of a funnel and use a paper-tube insert as the stem. If possible, give each child a funnel as a reminder of the lesson.

Lesson

The aspects of the mind discussed in this lesson are the conscious, the subconscious, and the superconscious.

Lead the discussion along these lines, adapting to the children's levels of awareness: "This funnel represents you and me.

We'll call it a symbol. The small stem represents our bodies. The large cone area represents our minds.

"The mind has two aspects or parts: the conscious part, of which we are aware, and the subconscious part, of which most people are unaware. These parts of the mind make up what we experience as consciousness.

"The narrow strip of tape next to the stem of the funnel represents the conscious mind—the part of the mind we think with. It senses, reasons, evaluates, and chooses. Because it can make choices, it is known as the decision-maker. Because it has the power to make decisions, it is the ruler of our physical lives.

"The rest of the mind, the much larger portion, is the powerful subconscious. It is exciting to know about because it does so many wonderful things for us. It builds, repairs, and operates our bodies. It is in charge of all our body processes, such as our heartbeat, blood circulation, digestion, and elimination. It is the storehouse of memory and the seat of emotion, habit, and instinct. But some things it does not do. It cannot think, reason, judge, or reject like the conscious mind does. Because the subconscious cannot do these things, it is under the control of the conscious mind. It can be compared to a computer, which is under the control of the computer programmer, the person who puts information into the computer."

With younger children, consider the analogy of a gardener planting seeds in the soil, which is comparable to the subconscious mind. "The soil accepts all seeds from the gardener, just as the subconscious mind accepts all suggestions or directions from the conscious mind. Now here's the good news: This phase of the mind has the ability to form. It can take any direction or belief our conscious minds give it and give that direction or belief form."

Offer examples from your experience. Think of times when you instructed your subconscious and, being the malleable substance it is, it formed according to your belief. Offer both negative and positive examples of your words or beliefs coming into existence. Suggest a simple experiment the children can test this on. A popular one is waking up so many minutes earlier than usual without the benefit of an alarm. Ask them to set their mental alarms ten minutes earlier for the following morning by saying as they go to sleep that they will be wide awake and eager to hop out of bed at that time.

Using the funnel again, explain: "The ability of the subconscious to form is unlimited because it opens up, like the funnel, to the great sea of mind, the formless stuff around us. This is the superconscious mind, the Universal Mind that knows everything and can answer our questions if we become quiet and really listen. We always have the choice between letting the limited conscious mind direct our computer mind or inviting in the unlimited, all-knowing power of the super-conscious that is waiting to respond to us. We do that by first asking and then quieting our conscious mind and listening within. Our superconscious mind can guide us much more accurately than the limited thinking and reasoning ability of our conscious mind can. That is why some people meditate or have a 'listening time' every day."

Many affirmations can relate to this lesson. They will enable the children to take more control of the decision-making ability of the conscious mind and to listen within to the superconscious. Remind the children that the subconscious will accept their habitual thoughts and give them form.

Suggested Affirmation
I think only of good things that I want to happen.

52
BELIEF ACTIVATES FAITH

This lesson has two analogies and could, therefore,
be divided into two lessons.

Materials

Two bowls or glasses, a piece of fish-tank hose or a bent straw
with one end placed in each glass or bowl, a glass of water, an
antacid seltzer tablet, and labels.

Lesson

Part 1: Faith is a power we all have. It's a continuous rhythmic
energy or vibration in every person's soul. Faith is the power
most directly involved in making the invisible visible.

Label one bowl or glass *Invisible World* and the other one *Visible World*. "There is an energy or substance in the invisible world out of which everything in our world has been formed. [Place the hose or straw between the two vessels and label it *Faith*.] It is faith that draws our good from the invisible to the visible. It is the power that says 'yes' to what has not been seen. It says 'yes' to Spirit, the one power that can produce our good.

"This power of faith is in all of us, but some people activate it and some don't. That's why it appears as though some people have faith and some don't. Unless our faith is activated or stimulated, it cannot draw forth our good from the invisible.

"Belief is what activates faith. This antacid tablet represents belief. Let's make a new analogy and say that the water in this glass is faith. That mighty power is lying dormant—asleep, inactive. It needs to be awakened or stimulated by our belief, our conviction."

Drop the antacid tablet into the glass of water. The tablet will cause the water to bubble or effervesce. "Now watch how alive and active faith becomes."

Part 2: An alternative belief analogy would be to use a siphoning action with the hose. The children could watch the water (substance) flow from the *Invisible World* container into the *Visible World* container via the hose *Faith*. Note that nothing happens until the flow is activated by belief. Otherwise, the water (substance) does not move. To start the siphoning process, submerge the hose in the *Invisible World* vessel that you have filled with water (substance). Cap one end with a finger and lift the hose out, placing it into the *Visible World* container, which needs to be on a lower level.

Affirmative statements can help build our belief system and strengthen our faith. Help the children to create simple declarations affirming belief in the Creator, belief in peace, belief in supply, belief in healing, belief in good. Ask them to exercise their faiths by looking toward the invisible world, not the visible world—toward cause, not effect. Offer some examples that would apply to the children's daily world.

Suggested Affirmation
I have faith in God, and I have faith in Good.

53
TUNING IN TO SPIRIT

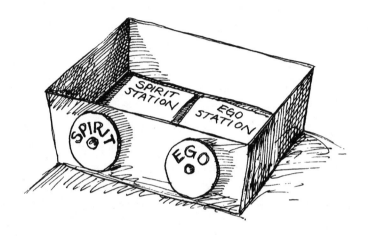

Materials

A shoebox, a piece of paper to fit neatly in the bottom of the box, a pencil, and a crayon for each child. Make two circles out of heavy cardboard for each box and put a paper fastener (brad) through the center of each so that you can fasten the circles to the box. The circles will be like radio dials. You may need a hole puncher to make the holes to attach the circles to the box. Nuts and bolts will work in lieu of paper fasteners.

Lesson

Tell the children that they're going to create a make-believe radio to help them listen to Spirit, or God. (Let's assume they're old enough to know that they won't hear a voice like on a real radio.) Discuss how there are always two voices inside us, two parts of our minds, that are vying for attention. One is the ego, sometimes called the "little self," and it always tries to speak up first. It gets so loud, we sometimes can't hear the other voice. Suggest that they take one of the circles, or radio knobs, and write *EGO* (Easing God Out) on it in big letters.

The other voice that tries to speak to us is God, or Spirit, or our Higher Self. Suggest that they print *Spirit* on the other circle in big letters. Hand each child a box to use for a pretend radio. "This is a radio you're going to look inside of, so you need to have the open side at the top." Using a hole puncher if needed, help attach the two knobs to their "radios."

"Radios often have both an AM and an FM dial. If a dial is tuned to an AM station, that is all we can hear. We can't hear an FM station unless we turn off the AM station and switch to FM. If we are listening to our ego, or our little self, that is all we can hear unless we're willing to turn off that station and turn on the station called Spirit. We can't listen to both stations at the same time, just as we can't hear AM and FM at the same time. We get to choose what to listen to because we have free will!"

If the children are older, ask how they can tell whether it's an AM or FM station that is playing. This can lead to a discussion regarding how they can tell when it's their little self or their higher self that is speaking.

Now ask the children to take the paper and draw a line down the middle. On the side where the *Spirit* dial would be, ask them to write *Spirit Station* as the heading, and on the other side, *Ego Station*. Underneath each heading, they will list clue words that will show which station they're listening to.

Proceed with a discussion to bring out such clues. They may say that there is a feeling of separation from others when ego is speaking, and a feeling of unity or oneness when they are tuned in to Spirit. In that case, they would put the word *sepa-*

ration in the *Ego* column and the word *unity* in the *Spirit* column. Or there is a feeling of certainty when listening to Spirit and much uncertainty, doubt, and confusion when hearing ego. Again, have them put the key words in the appropriate column. With Spirit, there is a feeling of joy, peace, and love. With ego, they may feel fearful, upset, or have attack thoughts. Someone may comment on the calmness felt when listening to Spirit and the frantic feeling when tuned in to ego.

Clue words and phrases should go in each column, but be sure they are at the children's vocabulary level or they won't serve their purpose as reminders.

"Ego tends to question and analyze; acceptance accompanies listening to Spirit. What about the guilty feelings that accompany ego versus the feeling of forgiveness of ourselves and others when we are tuned in to Spirit? Ego relieves problems but doesn't cure them; Spirit cures them completely. Spirit brings a practical solution, one in which everyone involved wins. Ego's purpose is to make conflict. The ego station is loud, but the Spirit station is usually very soft, unless you are a willing listener." Add more clues to the lists as you and the children think of them.

An appropriate ending for the session would be tuning in to Spirit via a listening meditation. This can be a non-specific meditation just to quiet the mind, or it could be for a specific purpose that concerns one child or the group.

"I hope you will put your shoebox radios in your bedrooms and look frequently at the lists to see what station you are tuned in to. Turn on a kitchen timer throughout the day, and when it rings, check to see if you have been listening to Spirit or to ego."

Suggested Affirmation
I choose to listen to the Spirit within, and I am guided in all I do.

54
OUR CUP OF BELIEF

Consider using this lesson after Lesson 50, "Belief Activates Faith."

Materials
Pencils, slips of paper, and an assortment of cups, glasses, and containers ranging in size from a thimble to a bucket.

Lesson
Our belief is the cup we hold for Spirit to fill with our good. Our good comes from invisible substance, and it is our belief that determines how much we will receive.

"All these vessels represent the size or amount of our belief in certain areas: our self-worth, our abilities, the experiences we'll have. Belief is made up of the thoughts and feelings that something is possible or not possible for us. For example, if we ask for a hundred dollars, but in our hearts we feel we'll only get twenty, that's our belief and that's what we'll get." Offer a couple of examples the children would especially relate to, such as going to camp, passing a test, or being accepted or invited somewhere.

On slips of paper, ask the children to write words about friendships, spending money, good health, trips, nice clothing, and specific abilities (piano playing, art, singing, typing, sports, and so on). Ask for areas of immediate concern. Write out the words for the children who are non-writers, and use colored slips of paper for the different categories.

Ask the children to decide just how much they really believe in each condition or experience, and then drop their slips of paper into each appropriately sized vessel. For instance, if they believe that they can have only a couple of friends, they would put their papers titled *Friendships* into a small vessel. If they believe a great many friendships are possible for them, they would put the slips into a much larger container.

The question, "How do we know what we believe?" may come up. Tell them, "When we want something, there is a small, quiet voice within that says something like 'That's not for you; you're not worthy' or 'You can do it; go for it!' This feeling or conviction is the belief that can cancel our desire or bring it to us.

"When we wish more good in any area of our lives, we must enlarge our cup of belief. We must rise above the feeling of unworthiness and know that true desires come from the Creator. Positive declarations or affirmations can help us start feeling worthy of greater good. Also, we might turn to Spirit and ask to have our beliefs expanded."

The lesson could end with a guided visualization exercise. Ask the children to choose an area in which they want to expand their beliefs in themselves. Guide them into a state of deep relaxation and have them visualize positive improvements in those areas.

Suggested Affirmation
I am a child of the Creator, and I deserve the best.

55
SEPARATING FEAR
AND THE PROBLEM

This lesson is intended for older children who can write and conceptualize easily. The lesson may be divided into two parts.

Materials

Part 1: A small box or shoe box, a piece of card stock labeled *Fear* placed facedown in the bottom of the box, slips of paper, and pencils.

Part 2: Eggs, a small cup or bowl, and an egg separator (a gadget used to separate the yolk from the white of an uncooked egg). The egg can be separated without the separator, but it is not as visually dramatic.

Lesson

Part 1: Hand the children pencils and slips of paper, and ask that they write, very briefly, some things that have irritated or angered them in the last few days. They may put several items on one slip or use a slip for each item. Assure them that no one will read the papers. When they are finished, ask them to crumple the papers and toss them into the box you have placed in the middle of the table.

"There is always an emotion hidden under anger or irritation. Can you guess what this emotion is?" Allow for responses, then remove the card from the bottom of the box and display the label *Fear*. Offer an example or two from your experience so they'll get the idea. You could say, "It irritated me when people told me what to do. Then I saw that the irritation was based on fear. I was fearful of others gaining control over me—of losing my freedom. Another time, it angered me when I was criticized in public. In searching for the hidden fear, I realized that I was afraid of losing friends, of being lonely."

Ask them to close their eyes and think about how their irritation or anger may have some fear hidden in it. Invite those who are willing to share examples of their anger and the fear they found under it.

Part 2: "Any time we have a problem or challenge in life, we can handle it more easily if we separate the fear from it. This egg symbolizes a problem. I'm going to pretend it's a problem I'm having with my mother. Now I'm going to separate my fears from the problem by using this egg separator."

Place the egg separator over the cup or small bowl. Crack the egg and let the yoke fall into the center of the separator and the white into the cup. "Watch the white, which symbolizes my fears, fall away into the cup. It feels so good to have all that fear separated from the problem so that it doesn't even feel as if there is a problem anymore. If there are only two basic emotions, love and fear, what do you think is left in the separator after all that fear has dropped into the cup? Love, of course! Love is the absence of all negative emotion. It is unconditional acceptance. With the fear separated from the problem or challenge and just love remaining, the solution is easy. Spirit is love, and this love provides the answer to any challenge in our lives. We can't hear solutions when fear is in our way. Fear can block our ability to listen to Spirit within."

In a small group or home setting, each child may like the opportunity to think of a challenge and then symbolically separate the fear from it with the egg separator. Use the eggs in an omelet or for baking a treat.

Suggested Affirmation
I am letting go of fear so that I can feel more love in my life.

56
IN-TO-ME-SEE
(INTIMACY)

Materials

A flashlight, a clear glass vase full of dirty water, and a jar full of clear water to flush out the dirty water.

Lesson

One of the Universal Virtues is transparency, which is being open, honest, and truthful about who you are to both yourself and others.

Show the glass vase filled with muddy water. "It is no longer transparent, is it? You can't see through it. This is how we are when filled with fear or worries, or are hiding parts of ourselves from others. Maybe we are hiding something we feel is wrong, or maybe we are hiding a part of us that yearns to be expressed, but we are afraid of the reactions of others. In either case, shining the Light of Love [use flashlight] on these areas will transform them and the circumstances around them, bringing about the virtue of transparency."

Pour clean water onto the vase of muddy water. "See this as the Universal Light of God pouring into our lives. Slowly but surely, the vase, like our lives, will become fresh and pure and transparent. It doesn't happen overnight and may require great courage, but being open and letting in the light can transform our lives forever." Be sure to allow talking time soon after this session.

Suggested Affirmation
I am open, honest, and transparent to others and myself.

57
JUST ONE PERSON CAN LIGHTEN DARKNESS

Materials

A candle, matches, and a darkened room. Optional: a candle for each child with a paper-skirt wax-catcher to protect hands from hot wax. Caution: Let the children hold lighted candles only if they are old enough to hold them straight.

Lesson

In a home setting, light one candle and eat by candlelight while the lesson is discussed. Observe how little light it takes to dispel darkness. Talk about how we have a choice in this world. We can choose to be like the candle and to lighten the darkness around us. Ask the children where they think darkness happens most frequently. Suggest that most of the darkness they will deal with will be in people's minds. This darkness is fear in its many forms: self-pity, anger, sorrow, self-doubt, jealousy, and thoughts of not having enough or of being adequate enough. Ask for examples of the forms of fear they've heard or seen. Ask how they can help bring light to such darkness. Discuss the ideas that you and the children develop.

If they come up with the idea of saying positive things to help another person, explain: "At times it may not be appropriate to speak, but we can think loving thoughts about unhappy people and picture them as happy once again. Picturing power is especially important when people are ill or injured. We can definitely aid them by visualizing them as healthy. But we cannot decide what someone needs in order to be well or happy. We only send our loving, light-filled thoughts. You might even visualize a bright, white light around the sad or ill person. This dispels darkness by creating a form of light that cannot be seen."

For additional discussion, demonstrate how just one person with a candle can lead the way through darkness, enabling others to follow. Let them follow you through the house. Point out how the light you carry stays behind and yet remains with you. The same is true with love. Suggest that they can be the candle bearers, and the candle they can carry is the truth about themselves and all others: that we are all of Spirit and are made in the perfection of the Creator can bring much light to dark minds. Offer some specific truths at their levels of awareness.

Optional: Have each child hold a small candle while you light each one from yours. Show how, when you give away some of the light from your candle by lighting each of theirs, there isn't less light because you've given some away—there's really more light. And that's also true when we share our love.

Suggested Affirmation
I am a child of the Creator, and I enjoy bringing light to others.

58
ANGER IS
SELF-DESTRUCTIVE

This lesson is intended for older children
who are familiar with knives and are not tempted
to experiment or play with them.

Materials
A kitchen knife displayed on a tray.

Lesson
Ask the children how they think it would feel if someone
picked up the knife by the blade. Then ask, "If that person
were to hit someone with the handle of the knife while holding the blade, who do you think would be hurt more? Anytime

we have hate and anger, it is just like holding a knife by the blade. In fact, someone once said, 'Hate is a weapon you wield by the blade.' Such emotions really hurt the one who has them and do not touch the other person unless he or she chooses to accept them.

"Anger is an attack upon oneself. It can clog the energy flow in the body. Because of the law of attraction, more anger or hate will come into that person's life. Remember: What goes out comes back after it gathers more of its kind.

"Anger is the Creator's love in us, imperfectly expressed. We can choose to redirect this energy, but first we may need to get these angry feelings out of us in an acceptable way. Some people have a firm pillow that they use as a punching bag. Or, when we feel full of irritation or attack feelings, we can take an imaginary paper bag and blow all those nasty, angry feelings into it. We can set it into an imaginary purple flame and let the flame consume all that negativity. Visualize the flame and affirm, 'I now let go of my anger and choose to be an expression of God's love.'"

Suggested Affirmation

I am a loving child of the universe, and I choose to see love in all others.

59
THE POWER OF THE WORD

This lesson is best used with older children
because of the capsules.

Materials
Three capsules (each one a different color) and a plate or
paper towel for each child. Buy empty capsules from the drug-
gist and fill some with a bland substance such as flour, some
with cayenne powder, and some with sugar.

Lesson
Hand each child a flour-filled capsule. "A word is a symbol of
an idea in the mind of a person. The words we use are like cap-

sules of thought and feeling. Words are creative and can form what we want or don't want depending on the thought and feeling in them."

Now have each child empty the capsule on a plate or paper towel. "This is the thought and feeling contained in a word. Moisten a finger and take a taste of the contents. How does it taste? Some of our words are also bland and don't have much creative power, such as 'It's nice weather today,' 'Let's go home,' or 'Where'd you put the butter?' These words do not contain much feeling. But there are a couple of words that are extremely powerful."

Hand out the cayenne capsules and have the children dump the "thought and feeling" onto their plates or paper towels. "Moisten a finger and taste the contents, but just a tiny bit because these words are full of power. How strong, sharp, and potent is the substance? It represents the words *I AM. I AM* is another name for God, so it is the most powerful creative statement we can say or think. Whenever we say *I AM*, we bring a lot of creative power to the thought or idea that follows it.

"When we say *I AM* with a lot of feeling, the universe responds and that condition comes into our lives unless we cancel it with opposite feelings. Our internal speech can be just as powerful as the spoken word. It is the feelings with which we charge the words that we must watch. '*I AM* sick and tired of this,' said with a lot of emotion, can cancel out '*I AM* a happy, healthy child of God' that is said without feeling. '*I AM* not liked,' said through tears, can cancel out '*I AM* a person others enjoy having around.'

"Because *I AM* represents our spiritual self, we must attach it only to positive thoughts." Encourage examples of such *I AM* sentences. A fun way of doing this is to play the *I AM* game. For each letter of the alphabet, someone offers an *I AM* statement ("*I AM* aware," "*I AM* brave," "*I AM* creative," and so forth).

143

Next, give each child a third capsule containing sugar or something else pleasant. Remind them that a word is a capsule of thought and feeling. Have them taste the contents and explain that it represents words that are sweet, loving, grateful, and uplifting.

There are few idle words. Most have the power to heal or to destroy. Talk about how the effect of a word can stay with us long after the sound of the word is gone. You may want to discuss the expression, "When the tongue speaks, the whole world moves." The things we say have a ripple effect that set joy or sorrow into motion. The children may wish to share some words they remember that have helped or hurt them a few weeks before.

Discuss words they could use that will uplift people. Encourage them to use words that represent only the very best thinking of which they are capable. End the lesson by speaking some uplifting words to each other—words of appreciation and gratitude.

Suggested Affirmation
The most powerful words I can say are I AM.

60
WEAVING OUR SPIRITUAL CONSCIOUSNESS

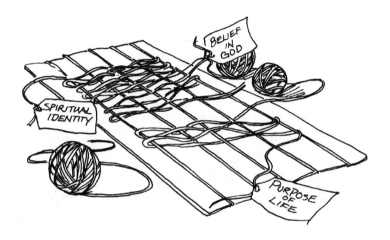

This lesson is best used with older children who have
developed some spiritual concepts.

Materials

Lengths of yarn in a variety of colors, a large-eyed, plastic yarn
needle, and a piece of sturdy hardware cloth (wire mesh) with
the edges bound by tape for you and each child. As an alternative, use a piece of cardboard with string wrapped around it to
form a warp. Small notches in the edges of the cardboard will
keep the string in place. Another option is to create dream-
catchers for this purpose. An alternative to a needle is to wrap
the last inch of yarn with some masking or cellophane tape

and to cut it at an angle to make a point. Other needle alternatives are a bobby pin or a pipe cleaner fastened to the yarn.

Lesson

"The piece of hardware cloth [or the cardboard] represents your individual consciousness, your collection of thoughts and feelings, or your total awareness, which is sometimes called the soul. We are going to talk about our spiritual awareness, the thoughts and feelings we have about spiritual matters. These are the thoughts that are woven into our consciousnesses and build our spiritual character. Sometimes we're not even aware of what our spiritual beliefs are, so let's try to identify them. We'll use these pieces of yarn to represent our thoughts, and we'll weave them into our consciousnesses [hold up the warp]. Let's first weave in our beliefs about the Creator. I'm going to use this pretty purple yarn for my belief."

Encourage the children to choose a piece of yarn to represent their ideas about the Creator and to thread it through the needle or pin. As they weave it in and out of the warp, ask them to verbalize their ideas—the feelings they have about what the Creator is or is not. You could begin by sharing your ideas (for instance, love, the one power, all-knowing, present throughout the universe, God, not a person, too vast to understand, and so forth).

These discussions are not guessing games in which only one answer is acceptable to you. This is a beautiful opportunity to hear the children's ideas, which may not be brought up if they feel they are being judged. Don't make it a right-or-wrong exercise, but an opportunity for you to note areas in which you may wish to offer instruction later. Sharing your thoughts while honoring theirs may be the best approach.

Next ask them to select a piece of yarn to represent who they think they are—that is, their spiritual identity (for instance, a child of God; a spiritual, mental, and physical being; a holy son or daughter of the Creator; a part of Spirit as a drop of water is part of the ocean; an expression of Source; an inheritor of spiritual gifts; a unique and special being).

The next strand of yarn represents their ideas of why they are here—the purposes of their lives (for instance, becoming my real self, the perfect person God created me to be, performing my part in the divine plan, my special function, expressing Spirit in my own unique way, learning the lessons I have chosen to learn in this lifetime, being truly helpful).

Use the next piece of yarn to represent the subject of our immortality or beliefs about death (for instance, there is no birth or death for the soul, life is eternal and we just change costumes, we can choose to live in many bodies to become as perfect as God wants us to be, death is a joyous experience).

Use another piece of yarn to deal with the nature of the universe and the world in which we live (for instance, everything in the universe operates by law and order or cause and effect, thoughts become things, we create our experiences by our thinking and feeling, there is only one power, it is a friendly universe).

Continue eliciting thoughts on other spiritual topics, such as prayer, meditation, heaven, angels, love, or whatever you deem significant. If the children are old enough, they may choose to make designs while they weave the yarn.

When all are finished, admire the results, reminding the children that each strand represents a spiritual idea and that this is how spiritual character is built. With older children, explain that consciousness precedes experience. The more that spiritual understanding is built into consciousness, the better one's life experiences will be.

One of the best ways to expand consciousness or to increase spiritual awareness is through meditation. Meditation is listening to Source, whereas prayer is talking to

Source. End the lesson with a time of silent meditation so that each may receive guidance from within.

You and the children may wish to make a "legend" to note on the back of the weaving which color yarn was used for which topic. Key words to remind them of their ideas could also be added. They may wish to hang the finished product on their bedroom walls.

Suggested Affirmation
I am growing in awareness as I listen each day to Spirit within.

61
MESSAGES FROM WATER

Materials

A bowl of water, a glass or paper cup of water for each child, and a small label or sticker for each glass or cup. If the children can't print, put *Love* and *Gratitude* on the stickers before the lesson. Try to have photos of water crystals (check with the library, bookstores, health food stores, and where calendars are sold).

Lesson

This lesson is inspired by the book *The Hidden Message In Water* by Masaru Emoto (Atria Books/Beyond Words, 2005). It includes many colored photos of remarkable water crystals.

Did you know your body is at least 70 percent water? To be sure the children understand 70 percent, show them a glass that is 70 percent full of juice or water. Get across that the human body is mostly water.

"Dr. Emoto, a scientist in Japan, has been studying water for many years and he has found that water makes beautiful crystals when shown positive words such as *Love* and *Gratitude*.

"One of Dr. Emoto's experiments was to freeze ordinary tap water, some of which was shown the words *Love* and *Gratitude*. The crystals formed from the ordinary tap water that had no exposure to *Love* and *Gratitude* was deformed and incomplete. But the same tap water exposed to *Love* and *Gratitude* formed crystals that were symmetrical, complete, and beautiful."

Have the children begin to consider how important water is in their lives. For instance, how bad it feels when they're thirsty, how good it feels to drink water, how much fun it is to go swimming, or how good it feels to take a shower or bath. Their bodies are made up mostly of water. Ask if they can then imagine how they might look or feel without having access to water.

You may have the children now place their *Love* and *Gratitude* stickers on their water glasses. You might also have the children express their gratitude by going around the circle and sharing out loud.

As part of the next part of the lesson, let them know that Dr. Emoto and his friends have, on more than one occasion, cleaned up very polluted lakes by standing around them and sending the water blessings of love and gratitude. Now you will use the bowl of water. Let it stand for one of the lakes that were cleaned up by people surrounding it and blessing it. Have the children close their eyes and imagine that they are present with Dr. Emoto and his friends at a polluted lake. How are they participating in their thoughts and feelings to make the lake clean?

Suggested Affirmation
Every time I use water, I bless it and offer it my heartfelt love and gratitude.

62
KEEPING CONNECTED TO SOURCE

Materials

A small table lamp, preferably without a shade; 25-, 60-, and 100-watt light bulbs; and an extension cord if needed. If you don't have a lamp, draw a picture or ask the children to use their imaginations.

Lesson

Point to the outlet where the lamp is plugged in. "We will call the outlet Source, and the lamp will be us. The cord will be our connection to Source, our pipeline to the pure, positive energy that flows from Source. The light bulb will represent the degree of our connection to Source, that is, the amount of positive energy flowing through us, the level of our vibration, the amount of light and love we are emanating."

Turn the light on with the 25-watt bulb in it. "The pure, positive energy is always flowing into us from Source, but with our free will, we have the power to disconnect from it. [Turn the light off.] How do we break our connection or block our energy flow? Judgment is one of the most common ways we block the energy flowing into our bodies. [Be careful not to judge their responses.] All negative emotions, which stem from fear, interrupt the flow of pure, positive energy."

Point to the lamp, which is still turned off. "Most people are like this light bulb: existing but not bringing light to the world. They are still plugged into Source [show the plug], because if they weren't, their bodies would not be alive. They have only blocked the pipeline to Source."

Ask the children how people might get the energy flowing again. Suggest that pure love, unconditional love for self and all others, is the greatest power in the universe. This love can break through blockages. "Unconditional love may be too big a step for many people, so what are some small steps these people can take? Appreciation or gratitude is one of the easiest. If people could find gratitude for all they have, for the people around them, and for the beauty they see, their lights would start shining. [Turn the light on.] But there are days when all of us become critical and selfish and angry, and guess what? We're not shining our light anymore. [Turn the light off.]"

While replacing the bulb with a 60-watt bulb, talk about how there are some people who spend time each day praying or listening for guidance from the Inner Teacher. These people have increased their capacities for light and love, and so their lights shine really brightly. Turn the light on.

Ask for ways people can open their hearts and show more love (for example, seeing more good in others and everything that occurs, trusting the Universe, feeling more love for oneself, forgiveness, not judging others). If it is not mentioned, bring up that service to others is one of the most powerful ways to keep connected to the pure love energy that is flowing from Source.

Turn the light off and explain: "Here is the switch of choice. Daily, we have the choice of how much of the Creator's love and energy we want to open up to and allow in. [Replace the 60-watt bulb with the 100-watt bulb.] We can decide if we want to block it with negativity or if we want to be a really powerful light on this planet. [Turn on the 100-watt light bulb.] Notice how much brighter this light is. It reminds me of some people on earth who are so committed to Source and to serving earth and its people that their light is brilliant. That is because they keep their connection strong and pure. Many have a daily silent sitting, meditation, or prayer time that keeps them tuned in to Source and their Inner Selves." Name some people in this category whom the children may know about.

Go back to the plug in the outlet. Remind them that they are always connected to Source, but they have a choice (the switch) as to how much of the pure, positive energy they want to allow in.

Optional: "Some people have a lot of light, but they keep it hidden. [Put a lampshade or a newspaper over the light bulb.] It's important that we let our light shine and not keep it hidden. The world is in great need of light right now."

Suggested Affirmation
I allow the energy of Spirit to flow through me, and I bless others every day.

A LESSON JUST FOR YOU

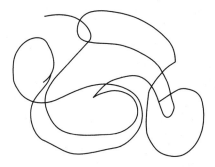

Each day, the Universe gives us a gift of pure energy. Our wise use of that energy is our gift back to the Universe. How we use that energy is colored by our consciousness, our awareness. The ideas presented in this book can help shift your consciousness enough that your energy will be filled with unconditional love and divine wisdom.

Each morning, visualize yourself making a scribble drawing to portray your daily gift of unadulterated energy. (You may wish to do this physically as a form of affirmation.) See yourself coloring the spaces with various thoughts and feelings. These colors represent your consciousness. May all your colors symbolize the love, joy, order, abundance, and harmony we're all working toward.

EPILOGUE

Now that you've read this far, you've absorbed a lot of universal principles—principles that work, just like gravity, whether we believe in them or not.

I feel that many young children intuitively know these truths, but they need parental support in fully remembering them. Consider creating a family support group around these ideas. Each week at a family meeting, select one lesson to focus on for the following week. You may choose it as a group, or each member may take a turn choosing one, or you may simply open the book at random.

During the week, give thought to that principle or exercise. Look for examples of it working in your life or in others' lives. Decide together what else seems appropriate to do with that lesson. Share questions, concerns, and examples at the next meeting.

You may even wish to have a daily five-minute support group around a lesson at the start of the day or at the dinner table. Support each other in remembering the principle, and then say the affirmation together. The support might sound

157

like this: "(Name), we unconditionally love you and support you in remembering (that your words have power)." Say this in unison with loving eye contact. Then tailor the affirmation as needed and say it together in unison also.

The more your children are reminded that there are spiritual and mental laws at work in this world and that through them they create their experiences, the less they will feel the victims of circumstance. They will have more control over their lives, a feeling of oneness with others, and inner joy. They will not so easily succumb to anxiety and fear, the two tremendous blocks to learning and to joy. Fear is usually False Evidence Appearing Real. The more our children understand the higher truths, the less they'll be affected by the false evidence that has seeped into mass consciousness and appears so real. Also, the more they'll be able to tap into joy—the energy of love that is their birthright.

Let's keep reminding our children that they are not just the forms we see, the body, but multidimensional spiritual beings here to enjoy a physical experience. It is our duty to turn them within, to their Inner Teachers, so they might get clear about their purposes here and the desires of their hearts. Then offer them the tools—the universal principles—to create their hearts' desires. When head and heart are in alignment, they'll know joy.

AFTERWORD

*Albert Einstein was once asked, "What's the most important
question that a human being needs to answer?"
He responded,
"Is the universe a friendly place or not?"*

It is intended that the preceding lessons will help children
understand that this is an orderly and benevolent universe. As
these lessons are modeled and discussed, our children will
indeed see this as a friendly place because it responds to the
thoughts they hold in mind.

The state of the world is a collective state of mind. As our
children understand the creative power of their thoughts as
well as the other universal principles, they will be playing a
part in healing our world. And please remember, our modeling
is more important than any lesson. We must embody the consciousness we want for them.

INDEX OF MATERIALS

L

labels, 124, 149
lamp, small for table, 152
lampshade, 154
lids, jar, 45
light bulbs, 152
liquid bleach, 48
loaf of bread, 17

M

magnet, 5, 45
magnifying glass, 5
marbles, 118
marker, washable felt, 45, 95
masking tape, 40
matches, 138
measuring spoon, 45
mirrors, 95
mobile, materials for, 114
Morning Glory, potted, 106

N

nail, 5, 45
needle, plastic yarn, 145
needle, sewing, 15
newspaper, 60, 98, 108, 110, 154
nutcracker, 45
nuts and bolts, 127

O

objects, assortment of, 55
onion, 84

P

pans, 104
paper
    carbon, 58
    carbonless, 58
    cardboard, 60, 64, 127, 145
    clip, 45, 95
    colored, 95
    cups, 67, 82
    funnel, 121

newspaper, 60, 98, 108, 110, 154
    scraps, 60
    scratch, 108, 110
    sheet of, 23, 38, 62, 127
    slips of, 130, 133
    in small pieces, 80, 89
    small wad, 101
    towel, 142
    wax-catcher, 121
    waxed, 114
paper, colored, 95
paper clip, 45, 95
paper cups, 45, 82, 149
paper funnel, 121
paper towel, 142
paper wad, 101
paper-skirt wax-catcher, 138
party horn, 19
pebbles, 48, 50. *See also* rocks; stones
pencils, 23, 58, 60, 89, 110, 127, 130, 133
pictures
    framed, 38
    from magazines, etc., 23, 98
    of reflection in water, 76
    of water crystals, 149
pipe cleaner, 146
plant, 68, 106
plastic yarn needle, 145
plate, 142
play dough, 112. *See also* clay
potato, 28
potato peeler, 45, 112
pots, 68, 112
pudding box, 104
pumpkin seeds, 53
puppets, 81, 85

R

recipes, 104
rice, packaged, 104

INDEX OF SUBJECTS